BLOCKADE

By the same author

The Scapegoat: The Life and Tragedy of a Fighting Admiral and Churchill's role in his death

The Coward? The Rise and Fall of the Silver King

Formidable

www.steverdunn.com

BLOCKADE

Cruiser Warfare and the Starvation of Germany in World War One

STEVE R DUNN

Seaforth
PUBLISHING

Copyright © Steve R Dunn 2016

First published in Great Britain in 2016 by
Seaforth Publishing,
Pen & Sword Books Ltd,
47 Church Street,
Barnsley S70 2AS

www.seaforthpublishing.com

British Library Cataloguing in Publication Data
A catalogue record for this book is available from the British Library

ISBN 978 1 84832 340 7

Typeset and designed by Mousemat Design
Printed and bound in Great Britain by CPI Group (UK) Ltd,
Croydon, CR0 4YY

CONTENTS

Dedication

To Vivienne, as ever, for unfailing support.

'Necessity can turn any weapon to advantage.'
Publilius Syrus (fl46–29 BC), *Moral Sayings*

'Beware the fury of the patient man.'
John Dryden, 'Absalom and Achitophel' (1681)

List of Illustrations

Plate section between pages 112 and 113

Dramatis Personae

It may be helpful to the reader to have to hand a quick reference guide to the roles of some of the players in this drama and their positions at the time.

Admiral Reginald Bacon: commanding Dover Patrol 1915–1918

Admiral Prince Louis Battenberg: First Sea Lord 1912–1914

Vice Admiral Lewis Bayly: commanding Queenstown and Western Approaches 1915–1919

Admiral Sir David Beatty: commanding Battle Cruiser Force 1914–1916, Commander-in-Chief Grand Fleet 1916–1919

Admiral Lord Charles Beresford: MP and retired admiral

Captain Hugh Brocklebank: captain HMS *Changuinola*

Admiral Sir George Callaghan: Commander-in-Chief Home Fleet 1911–1914

Rt Hon Winston Churchill: First Lord of the Admiralty 1911–1915

Rear Admiral Sir Christopher Cradock: commanding 4th Cruiser Squadron

Commander Selwyn Day: captain HMS *Dundee*

Rear Admiral Sir Dudley de Chair: commanding 10th Cruiser Squadron 1914–1916

Commander (later Captain) George England: captain HMS *Orvieto*

Admiral of the Fleet Lord John (Jacky) Fisher: First Sea Lord 1904–1910, 1914–1915

Sir Eric Geddes: First Lord of the Admiralty 1917–1919

Commander Francis Grenfell: HMS *Cedric*

Admiral Sir Frederick Hamilton: Second Sea Lord 1914–1916

Admiral Sir Henry Jackson: Chief of Staff, Admiralty 1913–1915, First Sea Lord 1915–1916

Admiral Sir John Jellicoe: Commander-in-Chief Grand Fleet 1914–1916, First Sea Lord 1916–1917

Vice Admiral Roger Keyes: commanding Dover Patrol 1918

Captain Francis Martin Leake: captain HMS *Achilles*

Midshipman Ernest McKeag: HMS *India*

Rt Hon Reginald McKenna: First Lord of the Admiralty 1908–1911

Lieutenant John Shuter: First Lieutenant HMS *Changuinola*

Rear Admiral Archibald Stoddart: commanding 5th Cruiser Squadron

Vice Admiral Reginald Tupper: commanding 10th Cruiser Squadron 1916–1917

Admiral Sir Arthur Wilson: First Sea Lord 1910–1911

16 March 1917

It was St Patrick's Eve. The sky was a mass of dull, pewtered grey: dark, lowering, and ominous. The constant stratus cloud was moving briskly to the northwest under the influence of a strong southeasterly wind. It was raining with a cold, biting determination broken only by the occasional resort to snow in squalls, blotting out the limited visibility. To the west lay the Shetland Islands, wind and storm tossed in unending winter; to the east Norway, with its ice and snow; and in between, a ship.

The ship was burning. A tall pall of smoke, bent over itself by the wind, hung over her. Jets of flame shot up through the plume, fierce orange, red and gold coloured against the gunmetal sky, like a Turner sunset in one of his late impressionistic masterpieces. The fore part of her hull was glowing red with inner heat, while oil poured from her ruptured tanks and settled around her, catching fire in places. She was Wagnerian, dying, a *Götterdämmerung* of steel and flame.

Over the vessel flew a Norwegian flag, red with a white-outlined Scandinavian cross. From her stern came the stilted popping of gunfire, the muzzle flash lost in the greater inferno of her immolation.

It was 1632 Greenwich Mean Time. One minute later the blazing ship rolled over onto her port side, exposing a clean, unfouled bottom and in a frenzy of roiled water, steam and fire sank down to the bed of the icy sea. Not one of the 325 men on board survived.

She was *Yarrowdale*; she was *Rena*; she was *Leopard*.

The Navy at War

The Royal Navy does not receive the same attention as the army for its activity in the First World War. No glorious Trafalgar swept the enemy from the sea and to his knees. No Quiberon Bay saved the country from imminent invasion. No Drake or Nelson took on the enemy in its own back yard. The year 1914 had been ridden with naval disasters – the escape of *Goeben* in the Mediterranean, the loss of *Audacious* and *Bulwark*, the sinking of *Bacchantes* off the Broad Fourteens, Coronel, and the loss of *Formidable* on New Year's Day 1915 all gave the impression of a service careless of men's lives for no apparent reason. Indeed, retired Admiral Lord Charles Beresford was moved to write to Admiral Sir Frederick Hamilton (then Second Sea Lord and in charge of personnel matters): 'the Navy will lose confidence in its leaders if officers and men are murdered without any particular object'.

Nor had it fulfilled its coastal defence role to the public's satisfaction. Scarborough, Whitby, Hartlepool and Great Yarmouth were shelled by Vice Admiral Hipper's battlecruiser force, leading to considerable loss of life and property and earning Hipper the soubriquet 'baby killer', without the navy exacting revenge.

The year 1915 brought no better, the botched battle of Dogger Bank being turned into a propaganda triumph despite manifold British failures. In 1916 the long awaited encounter between German and British battlefleets resulted in the inconclusive battle of Jutland (31 May) in which British losses of men and materiel were greater than those inflicted on the Germans. But as Arthur Balfour said at the time, 'before Jutland, as after it, the German Fleet was imprisoned; the battle was an attempt to break the bars and burst the confining gates; it failed and with that failure the High Seas Fleet sank back into impotence'. The years 1917 and 1918 saw no major naval actions, as the Germans showed no appetite for further encounters and stayed in port, mouldering away at anchor, an inactivity which eventually proved a fertile accelerant for the growth of Bolshevism and anarchy.

Meanwhile, on the Western Front an unparalleled slaughter was taking place as British, French and German soldiers alike were consumed by the sacrifice to Moloch and previously little known rivers, villages or towns – such as Mons, Ypres, Menin, Verdun, Somme – passed into the realms of infamy. British and Commonwealth losses of men in the period 1914–1918 were over one million, with another two million wounded. In comparison, the navy lost only 34,656 men (43,244 if the Royal Naval Division is included) with 5,158 wounded. 'What exactly was the navy doing in the war?' was the refrain of many both at home and in the trenches.

This was to miss the point. Apart from its offensive duties, the task of any navy is to keep the sea-lanes open for the importation of goods into its mother country; and equally to deny and interdict trade to its enemy. This was the unglamorous and uncongenial job the Royal Navy carried out for four long years. In quotidian unheard-of actions and patrols, largely unrecognised, often dull, seldom less than dangerous, the navy kept the vital arteries of trade open, despite strategic mishaps such as the delay in the introduction of convoy, and – equally importantly – denied freedom of the seas and of trade to Germany and her allies. By the concluding days of the war, Germany was starving – literally starving – to death. The pressure for an armistice by Germany in 1918 was as much driven by losses and stalemate on the battlefields as it was by the collapse of morale and order at home. Hunger stalked the land, anarchy and Bolshevism followed in its wake and soldiers, seeing that their kith and kin were in no way benefitting from their own sacrifices in the trenches, lost both the will to fight and their confidence in the Kaiser, court and general staff. And this hunger was because of the British naval blockade, maintained throughout the seasons and years, which crippled German industry and reduced food supplies to starvation levels.

The German navy, too, had started the war with a strategic intent to disrupt and destroy the trade of its opponents through the use of surface raiders. But it found success hard to achieve until the introduction of unrestricted U-boat warfare in 1917. The Royal Navy was able to seek out and destroy German commerce raiders and keep the trade routes free for British commerce.

This book tells that story and the story of the blockade of Germany. But more than that, the pages that follow tell how the Royal Navy significantly contributed to the winning of the war by the Allied forces, through denying Germany access to the sea, to trade and to vital raw and war resources; and how the German assault on British trade was contained until the unrestricted submarine warfare of 1917. It does so by considering, inter alia, the ships, men and activities of the 10th Cruiser Squadron in the northern seas and how they fought to keep the sea-lanes free for British trade and prevent the Germans gaining access to vital war materiel, and the German *guerre de course* at the beginning of the conflict. And this book culminates with the tale of one single action towards the end of this long campaign: like all the others little known about now or at the time.

The focus is on the use, by both sides, of civilian vessels: passenger liners and cargo ships, vessels never intended or designed for use in war but pressed into service, due to strategic failings in earlier times, as Armed Merchant Cruisers (AMCs) and sent to fight for their *patria* on the high seas, often against more suitably-armed and equipped regular naval units

The claim that the naval interdiction of German supply lines considerably helped to win the war is not to decry the massive contribution of those who gave their lives in the Allied cause on the Western Front and other battlefields. But without the trade blockade, the fighting would have gone on longer, the death toll been even higher and the eventual result less predictable.

The Royal Navy did not get to fight the new Trafalgar that it and the public so much desired, though such an action may not have been without grave risk. As Winston Churchill wrote, 'Admiral Jellicoe [the Commander-in-Chief of the Grand Fleet] was the only man on either side who could lose the war in an afternoon.' But the navy did win a hidden and possibly more valuable war – and one the Germans also wanted to win – the war on trade. This is its story, eventually crystallised into a single action in the North Sea. It is the story of the war on British trade, the Northern Patrol and the blockade of Germany; of the men (mostly volunteers) and ships of the 10th Cruiser Squadron who formed the barrier to German trade and raiders; and it is a memorial to the sailors who died in a single action near the North Pole. Theirs was an unsung and unseen war, but a vital one nonetheless.

As Marx and Engels observed: '*History* does nothing, it possesses no immense wealth, fights no battles. It is rather man, real living *man* who does everything, who possesses and fights.'

Foremost, this is a book about men.

PART ONE
The German Auxiliary Cruiser *Guerre de Course*

Recognising the importance to Britain of imported goods, the Imperial German Navy set a strategic goal to disrupt and destroy British trade. To accomplish such a task, the planners acknowledged that their limited number of appropriate vessels, essentially long-range cruisers, was insufficient. Thus they looked for other solutions. Britain, too, had a strategic imperative to disrupt and deny German trade; but first she had to determine the appropriate tactics.

1

A Change of Strategy, 1914

Given that Britain is an island with a prevailing westerly wind and with its most likely enemies off its eastern coast, separated by the North Sea and the Channel, close blockade of an opponent's ports to deny him access to the sea and trade was always going to be the navy's favoured strategy.

In the eighteenth and nineteenth centuries such a strategy proved successful, particularly against France. To take but one example from many, during the Seven Years War of 1754–1763, Louis XV's plan of invasion was ruined and his fleet destroyed by the close blockade of Admiral Hawke and others. In September 1759, for instance, Hawke himself was deployed off Brest, Duff off Morbihan, Rodney off the Normandy coast and Commodore Boys positioned off Dunkirk, while cruisers watched the Flanders coast and others watched Le Havre. The French fleet was bottled up, its invasion barges eventually destroyed and its ships put to the sword by Hawke at Quiberon Bay. As the historian Frank McLynn put it, 'the blockade was hurting the French badly as they later admitted. Even at the simplest level their matelots were cooped up in inaction and inertia while constant vigilance kept the Royal Navy at a high pitch of readiness'.

The Royal Navy was an inherently conservative institution whose motto could well have been 'if it ain't broke, don't fix it', and as it entered the twentieth century the navy saw no need to change a proven strategy. Close blockade and gunnery engagement at short ranges had worked for Nelson and Hawke, so there was no perceived need to change. When First Sea Lord Admiral Sir Arthur

'Old 'Ard 'Eart' Wilson was called to present the navy's strategy in the event of war to the Committee for Imperial Defence in 1911, his shambolic and muttered testimony implied that they would keep close blockade on the enemy's coast and engage his ships in the North Sea if they tried to come out. There was no mention of co-operation with the army, or any more ingenious strategy which might reflect the requirements of modern warfare and diplomacy, nor any consideration of the changes which new and different classes of ship might have wrought, an omission which earned him the sack (along with his political boss, First Lord of the Admiralty Reginald McKenna) and propelled the young and mistrusted Winston Churchill into the First Lord's chair.

In fact, voices had been questioning the accepted wisdom for some years. The deployment of large and costly warships in the North Sea and close to the enemy's coast had become, in some eyes, a much more perilous strategy, given the invention of the locomotive torpedo (invented by the British engineer Robert Whitehead in 1866 but initially rejected by the Royal Navy), the submarine, the mine and the torpedo gunboat. Now small, low-cost weapons, available to any tin-pot country, could be used to damage or sink expensive capital ships, especially in the confined waters of the coastal littoral or the narrow North Sea. The refusal of many in the Admiralty to recognise this game-changing fact was in part ignorance, part snobbery and part a recognition that all their expensive hardware and accepted strategies would be at naught if submarines and torpedoes ruled the roost.

Submarines were seen as a much reviled and distrusted class of ship. Many sailors thought them a dishonourable and underhand weapon, suitable only for weaker nations and only then for coastal defence. Sir Arthur Wilson, as an example, thought that their crews should be hanged as pirates if captured and while in office as First Sea Lord did much to retard the development of the weapon for the Royal Navy. In 1911 the Inspecting Captain of Submarines (the man in charge of the navy's submarine development and training) was Captain Sydney Hall. He was a man of firm opinions and at odds with Wilson on tactical matters, particularly the pace of building new submarines and the type of boat which should be built. When it appeared to Wilson that Hall was getting too close to the engineering companies building the navy's submarines, Wilson took the opportunity to fire him from his post and assigned him to an old and useless third-class cruiser, *Diana*, based off Crete.

It was the tradition that the departing officer had the right to nominate his own successor, and Hall nominated Captain Frank Brandt, a navy 'brain', and at the time in charge of the 8th Submarine Flotilla. Wilson overruled this appointment and appointed the more congenial Roger Keyes instead. But Wilson's desire to impose his own will on submarine development did not stop there. Brandt, a submarine specialist, never got another decent posting; he was assigned first to an old (1894) and wretched second-class protected cruiser, *Eclipse*, and in July 1914 to *Monmouth* – then in the Third Fleet – and took her to die a fiery death at the battle of Coronel on 1 November 1914. The general attitude of most senior officers of the period could be summed up by the comments of Brandt's admiral at Coronel, Rear Admiral Sir Christopher Cradock, to his friend Roger Keyes, the new Inspecting Captain of Submarines, 'it would be far more satisfactory to these "playthings" to know whether they were observed or made hits or misses … I am sure you will know what to do'. 'Playthings' was the common view.

But one man who clearly saw that submarines had revolutionised naval warfare, and hence the strategy of close blockade, was Jacky Fisher, quondam First Sea Lord, and the man who created the dreadnought. Fisher had driven the introduction of submarines, and when out of office continually badgered First Lord Winston Churchill to increase the numbers being built. More than anyone, Fisher realised that the advent of the torpedo-armed submarine meant that the narrow waters of the North Sea and English Channel became a very high-risk environment for large and expensive capital ships. Rather than risk battleships in such a situation it was better, he argued, to police those waters through 'flotilla defence', using large numbers of torpedo boats (surface vessels carrying on-deck torpedoes), submarines and torpedo boat destroyers (more usually abbreviated to 'destroyers') to render the waters uninhabitable for enemy battleships, potential invasion fleets and the like. Fisher's was something of a lone voice in the wilderness for much of the early part of the twentieth century, although he was not without support. Rear Admiral Frederick E E Brock, commanding the Portsmouth Division, Home Fleet, wrote to the then First Lord, McKenna, in March 1910, referring to the recently published Naval Estimates for 1910–1911 and insisting 'how much I think that the additional men and destroyers provided for are required in addition to the battleships'.

Under pressure from Fisher, Churchill began to consider the possibilities of 'flotilla defence', whereby large numbers of light (and cheap) craft would be deployed in the North Sea, with the battlefleet held to the north to intervene when the enemy was 'fixed', and the implications of this on a strategy of close blockade. Not the least of the attractions of such a scheme for Churchill was its economy and his need to stabilise the naval cost estimates. With this in mind, in February 1912 he asked his Chief of the Naval Staff, Rear Admiral Ernest Troubridge, to work on a plan for a North Sea deployment that would adopt the idea of using light forces. This plan was ready to issue to the Commander-in-Chief Home Fleet by May, but a last minute intervention by Churchill, demanding that it be tested in manoeuvres, stopped its issue (and infuriated Troubridge).

When tested in the summer, the fleet manoeuvres showed the scheme to be seriously flawed. Troubridge's war plan was a compromise between close blockade and flotilla defence and as such satisfied no one. He proposed a cordon of three hundred miles from Norway to the Dutch coast – an intermediate blockade, as opposed to the close blockade planned for in 1911 and for many years beforehand. This was shown to be unworkable, for the navy did not have enough cruisers or destroyers to support it. Churchill was forced to make an embarrassing climb-down in front of the Committee for Imperial Defence. He blamed Troubridge and soon got rid of him.

For the public at large, the major concern was not of the intricacies of flotilla defence, but of invasion. It is strange that, in the years leading up to the war, Britain and its politicians were seized by the thought of invasion and much argument was expended concerning the need to retain soldiers at home to deal with this threat, rather than send them to France, and as to where the navy should be stationed to meet it. Books such as Erskine

Childers's *The Riddle of the Sands* (1903) and *The Invasion of 1910* by William Le Queux, serialised by the *Daily Mail* in 1906, had stoked such fears, as had Guy du Maurier's play *An Englishman's Home* of 1909, which ran uninterrupted for eighteen months. In 1908 the Committee of Imperial Defence had appointed an invasion inquiry before which former Prime Minister A J Balfour, amongst others, testified. The conclusion was that a successful invasion could not be mounted, but the public were not aware of this and the 'idea of invasion became almost a psychosis'. In reality, the Germans had no such plans and had never had such plans – it was a complete red herring.

But other, more perceptive, voices began to see another threat, that of the danger to our supply chain. In July 1914 Sir Arthur Conan Doyle wrote a short story for *The Strand Magazine*. It was billed as 'the amazing story of England's peril and how our naval supremacy was challenged by a few submarines'. In Conan Doyle's tale he has an enemy naval officer make this speech:

> of course, England will not be caught napping again in such a fashion. Her foolish blindness is partly explained by her delusion that her enemy would not torpedo merchant vessels. Common sense should have told her that the enemy will play the game that suits them best – that they will not inquire what they may do but they will do it first and talk about it afterwards. The opinion of the whole world now is that if a blockade were proclaimed one may do what one can with those who try to break it and that it was as reasonable to prevent food from reaching England in war time as it is for a besieger to prevent the victualling of a beleaguered fortress.

Reviewing the story, the *Daily Telegraph* asked retired Admiral Lord Charles Beresford for an opinion. He ventured, 'we have done something to meet the dangers to our food supplies by arming some of our merchantmen', which was technically true, as plans existed for that to happen in time of war. The writer Arnold White (author of *The Navy and its Story*) added that Sir Arthur has 'placed his finger on the neuralgic nerve of the British Empire – ie the precarious arrival of our food supplies'.

The recognition that food and raw material supply was critical to any war effort was not uniquely Conan Doyle's. It had been articulated as early as the sixteenth century by Sir Walter Raleigh who wrote, 'there are two ways in which England may be afflicted. The one is by invasion … the other by impeachment of our trades'. As then, as now.

With regard to the fragile nature of the supply chain to the British Isles, it is worth noting that this issue had been addressed by Parliament at least five times during the Dutch and Napoleonic wars of the seventeenth, eighteenth and nineteenth centuries. The Compulsory Convoy Act of 1798, for example, compelled all British merchant ships to and from British ports in time of war to sail in convoy, protected by Royal Navy ships, and in return for the payment of a fee for the protection provided. This act was not repealed until 1872, pressure from the shipowners being the driving force. This repeal was in fact a major change in war strategy for the Royal Navy, although this was little recognised at the time. The navy's role was now defined by phrases such as 'securing the sea communications', 'protecting the ocean highways' and 'preserving the sea routes': all phrases which hid the fact that merchant ships would no longer receive direct protection. This would be a significant problem when war came.

*   *   *

Rear Admiral Troubridge was exited from his post at the end of 1912 and new war plans were issued to the Commander-in-Chief Home Fleet, Admiral George Callaghan, for 1913. These plans enjoined him to base himself on the Firth of Forth and 'sweep and patrol' the southern half of the North Sea with his fleet, without specifying the extent of such sweeps or their frequency, but ordering him not to pass beyond a point roughly halfway across. Callaghan was informed that 'the general idea of these plans is to exercise economic pressure upon Germany by cutting off German shipping from Oceanic trade'. The penny had dropped, although not with everyone. Rear Admiral David Beatty, for one, wrote to Churchill, whilst still serving as his naval secretary, to complain about both the vagueness and the lack of offensive spirit in the new orders. Churchill proved to be a waverer, advocating in 1913 a madcap scheme for close blockade of the Heligoland Bight and the capture of the island of Borkum. Callaghan was dismissive: 'this policy of close blockade was considered a few years ago and abandoned as impractical. As it appears to be still more impractical now it is useless to consider it', he wrote. Churchill continued to press for his plan as late as June 1914, however, ignoring the inconvenient realities.

Thus it came about that, under a possibly reluctant Churchill, and successive First Sea Lords (he got through four), the navy developed a plan which took account of the changed realities of naval warfare. Out went the concept of close blockade and engagement of the enemy's battlefleet close to their shores. In came the idea of distant blockade and the slow strangulation of an opponent's power to resist. As war against Germany was declared, the British Grand Fleet sped to its haven of distant Scapa Flow in the Orkney Isles; the Channel Fleet of old and expendable battleships assembled at Sheerness to escort the BEF to France and defend against the much-feared invasion; and smaller ships assembled at Dover, Harwich and in the Orkney and Shetland Islands to create the northern and southern limits of a distant blockade, closing the North Sea entrances and exits to Germany and its allies.

2

Cruiser Warfare

The interdiction of an enemy's trade on the high seas had always been a major facet of naval warfare. Whether it be Drake and Raleigh, licensed privateers plundering Spanish ships for the Virgin Queen in the sixteenth century, or Joseph Barss in the *Liverpool Packet* capturing fifty American vessels in the war of 1812, the disruption of an opponent's trade was seen as a legitimate (and profitable) activity.

For most of the nineteenth century the British considered that their most likely opponent at sea would be the French, and vice versa. However, the French also observed that they were deficient in heavy ships (battleships) and unlikely to make up the deficit for reasons of cost and resources.

Out of this strategic conundrum was developed a new concept known as the *Jeune École* (Young School). Its adherents advocated a two-pronged strategy: first, the use of small, powerfully equipped units to combat a larger battleship fleet, and secondly, commerce raiders capable of ending the trade of the rival nation. Without overtly saying so, the plan was clearly aimed at Britain, the largest navy in the world at the time and heavily reliant on trade for economic prosperity and survival.

The French developed and commissioned a new class of vessel specifically designed as raiding ships for this role, such as *Dupuy de Lôme*. Laid down in 1888, but with typical French lassitude not commissioned until 1895 – by which time her originality had been lost – she was capable of 23 knots, and intended to raid enemy commerce ships during extended cruises.

She was the first true armoured cruiser, superior to existing British protected cruisers, especially in her relatively thick steel armour. She could control the fighting range with her superior speed and her heavy armament of multiple-calibre quick-firing guns, all of which were mounted in gun turrets which contrasted with her putative opponents, where guns were mounted in lightly protected casemates or pivot mounts.

Such strategic thinking exerted a considerable influence on the development of smaller navies during the century, particularly as they tried to compensate for weaknesses in battleships. These developments were not lost on German navy planners either, especially the aspect of a war on trade.

So it was that both Britain and Germany approached the war with this strategic intent of a war on commerce in mind. For Britain, the navy had not just to bottle up the North Sea but also had to both prosecute actions against German trade worldwide and protect British merchant shipping from interdiction by enemy raiders. Neither country was self-sufficient in food or vital war materials, and both assumed that the other could be severely incapacitated by a successful cruiser warfare campaign.

Cruiser warfare was planned to be conducted under so-called 'prize rules'. These, originally drafted at the Treaty of Paris in 1856 and subsequently re-ratified at the Hague Conventions of 1899 and 1907, stated in essence that passenger ships could not be sunk, crews of merchant ships were to be placed in safety before their ships could be sunk (lifeboats were not considered a place of safety unless close to land) and only warships and merchant ships that were a threat to the attacker might be sunk without warning.

The Treaty of Paris also gave legal basis to the concept of blockade. The agreement, among other things, permitted 'close' but not 'distant' blockades. A belligerent was allowed to station ships near the three-mile limit to stop or inspect traffic with an enemy's ports; it was not allowed simply to declare areas of the high seas comprising the approaches to the enemy's coast to be off-limits. Britain ignored this treaty in 1913, when it determined that its strategy against Germany would henceforth be based on a distant blockade.

Goods not permitted to pass through a blockade were designated as contraband. The definition of contraband was established by the

Declaration of London in 1909 (and which Britain, in fact, never ratified). Three definitions of contraband were established: one of 'absolute contraband', namely, articles which were clearly war materials; and another deemed 'conditional contraband', which comprised articles capable of use in either war or peace. This 'conditional' list included items such as ore, chemicals and rubber, all of which were becoming increasingly important to any modern war effort. The third category was a 'free list', containing articles that could never be deemed contraband.

Following the lead of the Hague Conference of 1907, the Declaration of London of 1909 considered food to be conditional contraband, subject to interception and capture only when intended for the use of the enemy's military forces. Among the corollaries of this was that food not intended for military use could legitimately be transported to a neutral port, even if it ultimately found its way to the enemy's territory. The starvation of an enemy's populace was therefore meant to be outlawed as a weapon of war. The House of Lords had refused its consent to the declaration, which did not, consequently, ever come into full force.

Jacky Fisher thought that the submarine changed the rules and made the international agreements irrelevant. In 1912, by then retired from the post of First Sea Lord where he had done much to bring the submarine into service, he presented a paper to the Cabinet. Fisher developed the argument that submarines would find adherence to prize rules impossible for a simple practical reason: a submarine could not capture a merchant ship, for it would have no spare manpower to deliver the prize to a neutral port; neither could it take survivors or prisoners, for lack of space: '... there is nothing a submarine can do except sink her capture'. If a merchant ship were armed, as was permitted by a conference in London in 1912, then a submarine was surely able to view her as a potential attacker and destroy the ship. Further, he asked, 'What if the Germans were to use submarines against commerce without restriction?'

His view did not gain favour. Winston Churchill, supported by senior naval opinion, said it was inconceivable that 'this would ever be done by a civilised power'. In this he was to be much mistaken.

To prosecute trade warfare, both the British and German navies thought that they would need cruisers to roam the seas, being the successor ship to the frigates of Nelson. These were long-range ships, designed to operate for considerable periods away from base and to defend themselves against similar antagonists, whilst being speedy enough to catch and destroy any prey. At the outbreak of war the Royal Navy had 108 cruisers, but at least half of them were obsolete and many had been decommissioned to the Third Fleet. Many more were unsuited to the job now required. In reality, only a few dozen were really appropriate for the task. In part this was because British cruiser design had gone down a dead end.

In 1888 a three-class system had been introduced, originally based largely on size, and influenced by the developments of the *Jeune École*. Armoured and first-class cruisers (many of which were still in use in 1914) were generally over 10,000 tons, and most carried two or more 9.2in guns and a large number of 6in or 7.5in guns. These were generally called 'armoured cruisers', but by 1914 were both unsatisfactory and obsolete as commerce raiders or for trade protection duties. Their size varied: the largest were as large and expensive as battleships, and often required a larger or similar size of crew owing to their need for more boilers (to give both speed and range) than a battleship, and at full speed they generally needed more stokers. Their need for considerable quantities of both men and coal made them less than useful in distant deployments. The surviving second- and third-class cruisers were distinguished mainly by their largest guns. The second-class cruisers generally all carried at least two 6in guns. The third-class cruisers carried 4in guns and were smaller ships.

The second-class cruiser went out of fashion after the *Highflyer* class of 1899–1900, and no new designs appeared until the *Bristol* class of 1909–1910. These ships saw the older triple expansion engines replaced by turbines and coal power substituted by a mix of coal and oil. They were known as 'light cruisers'. While the *Bristol*- and *Weymouth*-class cruisers only carried deck armour, the *Chatham*-class cruisers of 1911–1916 carried a belt of armour on the waterline. Light cruisers were excellent ships and ideal for commerce interdiction and protection. But they were also in great demand to serve with the Grand Fleet, acting as 'the eyes of the fleet', and were in short supply for other duties as a result.

There were also 'scout-class' cruisers, very lightly built and of short range, carrying even smaller guns than the third-class cruisers. They were sometimes used as 'destroyer leaders', but were eventually superseded by the increasingly seaworthy destroyers, whose faster speed made them much better and rather less expensive.

Jacky Fisher inherited much of this confused thinking when he became First Sea Lord in 1904. At that point there were fifteen classes of first-class cruisers including the *Shannon* class, the last Royal Navy ironclads to be built, which had a propeller which could be hoisted out of the water to reduce drag when under sail, and ten other classes of second-class vessels.

What is more, he knew that the Germans planned to use their fast passenger liners such as *Wilhelm der Grosse* and *Kaiser Wilhelm* – capable of 21 and 23 knots respectively – as 6in-gunned trade interdiction cruisers. At these speeds no British cruiser could catch them.

His response was twofold. First, to scrap 154 cruisers, sloops and other vessels 'too weak to fight, too slow to run away'; and secondly, to introduce the super-cruiser, originally known as a Large Armoured Cruiser (LAC) which would combine high speed with heavy gun armament. These were the *Invincible*-class ships, 25.5 knots and eight 12in guns, launched in 1907. They made all other cruisers obsolete. The LACs were predators, able to outrun anything which had heavier arms and outshoot anything which could match their speeds. They were intended to work in pairs attached to a light cruiser squadron, hunting down enemy cruisers and protecting British trade. It was not until 1913 that they became regarded as the fast arm of the Grand Fleet (under Beatty's urging) and were thus thrust into the line with the battleships – a role for which neither their design or armour protection equipped them – and were now commonly called 'battlecruisers'. And so when war came, they were not allocated to the duty intended (except once at the battle of the Falkland Islands) and the paucity of the Royal Navy's cruiser resource was once more thrown into sharp focus.

The consequence of this rather scattergun approach to cruiser design was that, despite the apparent numerical strength of the British cruiser force, the reality was a shortage of useful vessels and the most versatile type – the light cruiser – was in demand everywhere.*

In order to make up the deficit, the Admiralty hit upon the idea of arming large passenger liners. These had the advantage of being generally speedy, and good sea boats able to stay on station for long periods. Their rather obvious disadvantage was that they were unarmoured, contained a lot of flammable material and presented a huge profile as a target to an enemy (*Otranto*, for example, attached to the 4th Cruiser Squadron on the outbreak of war, was nicknamed 'The Floating Haystack'). Designated Armed Merchant Cruisers (AMCs) and armed with old and surplus 4.7in and 6in guns, they were pressed into service to fill the gap. Fisher was a fan, stating that 'large mercantile vessels are the best scouts', but he was in the minority.

Passenger liners were requisitioned by the Royal Navy for conversion at the beginning of the war. Initially, it was intended to include the very largest ocean liners, such as *Aquitania* and *Mauretania,* but it was found that their huge size precluded them from practical employment. The logistics involved in their heavy fuel consumption and in providing suitable ports for refuelling and resupplying was very limiting. Additionally, their massive silhouettes made them easily recognisable from long distances. *Mauretania,* although converted and armed, was never commissioned as an AMC, while *Aquitania* was commissioned for two weeks, which ended after she collided with the steamer *Canadian* in August.**

The German navy, always at a quantitative disadvantage versus Britain, had hit upon the idea of arming passenger liners as far back as 1895. They had developed elaborate plans to put a large number

* To illustrate the extent of this confusion, in 1914 the Royal Navy had twelve designated cruiser squadrons (although one had no ships in it), all of which were based around, or entirely comprised of, armoured or first-class cruisers. By 1918 there was only one armoured cruiser squadron left in commission (the 2nd) and light cruiser squadrons comprised the majority of the cruiser force, the older and bigger ships having been retired to depot or base ship status.

** In 1906 Cunard launched *Lusitania* and *Mauretania,* both capable of an average speed of 24 knots. The British government had made a loan to Cunard of £2,400,000 at 2.75 per cent interest for the ships. They were stiffened to carry 6in guns and had an annual operating subsidy of £75,000 per ship, in addition to the mail subsidy.

of such ships into service, calling them *Hilfskreuzer*. However, the outbreak of war had caught the Kaiserliche Marine on the back foot and they had only three large passenger liners in the North Atlantic. Coupled with Vice Admiral Graf von Spee's armoured cruiser force at Tsingtau and the light cruisers *Karlsruhe* in the Caribbean and *Königsberg* in German East Africa, these ships formed the entirety of the German commerce-raiding force at the commencement of hostilities (although they did have twenty-one submarines in home waters). It was to prove impossible for them to add to these ships in the early months of war, as the British distant blockade denied them access to the high seas and their passenger liners, well known before the war, were impossible to disguise as anything other than themselves.

The Royal Navy, in fact, credited the German programme with more success than it achieved and was convinced that, at the outbreak of war, every American Atlantic port would hold a German *Hilfskreuzer* ready to mount its guns and prey on British trade. Admirals Cradock and Stoddart, with the 4th and 5th Cruiser Squadrons respectively, were deployed off the eastern coast of the Americas and the mid-Atlantic to counter this perceived threat.

And so both sides went to war on each other's vital trades with a mixture of the obsolete and obsolescent, the mongrel and the unlikely. This was cruiser warfare in 1914.

3

The Escapee, 1914

Many German vessels which might have had a role in cruiser warfare found themselves in British ports at the declaration of war and were interned. One such was the Hamburg-Amerika liner *Belgia*, en route from Boston to her home port, in want of coal and earmarked for AMC duty. She had tried to put into Newport to coal on 4 August but was refused by order of the Admiralty and anchored off Ilfracombe instead. *Belgia* became possibly the only liner to be arrested by the police. On 5 August the Newport harbour master, accompanied by the town's chief of police and twelve rifle-armed policemen, boarded her and took her to Newport docks where she was interned. She had seventy-three German reservists bound for the army on board, as well as £250,000 of foodstuffs and some animals consigned to Hamburg Zoo, including two alligators.

Neither could the liners in German ports which were earmarked for an AMC role make it through the British blockade. The only German liner to successfully put to sea as a raider from a home port in Germany was *Kaiser Wilhelm der Grosse*. She escaped the blockade by sailing from Bremen on the day war was declared, and before the Northern Blockade was fully in place, and went around the north of Iceland before heading for an area off the Canary Islands. Her short career was dominated by a desperate need to find coal.

Kaiser Wilhelm der Grosse was a transatlantic ocean liner named after Wilhelm I, German emperor and the first ruler of united Germany. Constructed in Stettin for the North German

Lloyd (NDL) company, she entered service in 1897, was the first liner to have four funnels, measured 14,349 tons (grt), was 655ft long and had a top speed of 22.5 knots.

The ship ushered in a new age of ocean travel and the distinction of having four funnels quickly became emblematic of size, strength, speed and luxury. In 1897, on her maiden voyage across the Atlantic, she made the fastest crossing yet recorded and gained the Blue Riband (awarded for the fastest Atlantic crossing to New York) for Germany, a prize which had been previously dominated by the British.

By 1914 she had lost her glamour and had been converted to take third-class passengers only. But now she was in the Imperial German Navy and loose on the high seas. She quickly captured two merchant ships and a trawler, sinking all three for a total of 10,683 tons but, in an act of chivalry which was distinguished in the war at sea by its singular character of mercy, stopped and released two passenger liners. Her captain, Reymann, was troubled by the large numbers of women and children on board. One liner to be so treated was *Galician*, which was intercepted on 15 August. After stopping her and ordering the passengers and their belongings on deck, and taking two soldiers – a lieutenant and a private – on board as POWs, the German ship ordered *Galician* to sail with her, covering her with the deck guns. At daybreak Reymann sent the signal, 'We will not destroy your vessel owing to the women and children on board. You are released. Captain.' 'Grateful thanks of passengers and crew' was the reply from the *Galician.*

Likewise, on 16 August *Kaiser Wilhelm* intercepted three British merchantmen. *Kaipara* and *Nyanga* were sunk after the 101 men on board them had been transferred to the German ship. The third ship, the Royal Mail steamer *Arlanza*, had women and children amongst her passengers. Reymann allowed her to go after she threw her wireless overboard. This chivalry would be the source of his undoing.

The German ship's need for coal took her to the African coast and the neutral Spanish waters of the port of Rio de Oro, a desolate Spanish anchorage on the Sahara coast, some three hundred miles south of the Grand Canary, then in the Spanish Sahara, now Dakhla, where German and Austrian colliers were expected, and where Reymann commenced coaling immediately on their arrival. Coaling a ship is an exhausting occupation, an all-hands evolution where everyone and everything gets covered in black dust. Coal is first hand-loaded into sacks in the collier, then the sacks are swung by hoist onto the deck of the receiving ship and finally deposited into the coal bunkers of the consignee vessel. It also causes a massive pile of dust which hangs in the air like the plume of a large fire and is a give-away signal to an observer that something is afoot. But Reymann felt relatively at ease, so much so that he had tarried there for nine days, waiting for his colliers and hoping for news of potential targets. He was after all, he thought, in neutral waters and no British ship would dare intrude on Spanish neutrality to reach him. It was 26 August, just twenty-two days after he had swept through the nascent British Northern Blockade.

The laws relating to neutrality gave belligerent ships the right to remain in a neutral harbour for only twenty-four hours, except when in need of urgent major repair, and only then for the purposes of taking on food, water and fuel. Clearly, Captain Reymann did not think that the Spanish would be over zealous in enforcing the law in this far-flung corner of their empire.

The old ship HMS *Highflyer* was a second-class protected cruiser launched in 1898. With a length of 373ft and displacing 5,550 tons, she was armed with no less than eleven 6in QF guns, together with eight 6pdrs and six 3pdr Hotchkiss guns. Each 6in weapon fired a projectile weighing 100lbs over about 10,000yds. Despite her age, she was a formidable weapons platform against a less well-armed opponent.

Her captain was Henry Tritton Buller, quondam flag lieutenant to Sir John (Jacky) Fisher, son of Admiral Sir Alexander Buller, the ex-Commander-in-Chief of the China Station in 1895, and whose family had owned estates around Morval in Cornwall since the fifteenth century. Henry, born in 1873, had been appointed a captain in June 1911 and two years later took command of *Highflyer*. His family lineage included several admirals and he was married to Hermione, the daughter of the 17th Earl of Moray, Morton Gray Stuart, who claimed descent from King James V of Scotland. Buller was a man of considerable self-confidence.

He had already had a 'good war'. In August 1914 *Highflyer* was allocated to the 9th Cruiser Squadron, under Rear Admiral John de Robeck, on the Finisterre station. She left Plymouth on 4 August and intercepted the Dutch ocean liner *Tubantia*, which was returning from South America when the war began, with £500,000 in gold destined for banks in London, a large proportion of which was intended for the German Bank of London. She was also carrying some 150 German reservists in steerage class and a cargo of grain destined for the German markets. Buller stopped her and, after boarding by an officer and crewmen from *Highflyer*, escorted the ship, money, men and cereal into port and captivity at Plymouth, where no doubt three of the four commodities were most welcome.

Highflyer then transferred to the Cape Verde station, in support of Rear Admiral Archibald Stoddart's 5th Cruiser Squadron which was hunting for *Kaiser Wilhelm der Grosse*, thought to be in those waters. With no certain knowledge of the German AMC's whereabouts, some luck was needed, but on 24 August the British consul at Las Palmas in the Canaries reported that on 17 August she had put into Rio de Oro. In company she had the steamship *Duala*, recently berthed in Las Palmas, and which, after staying forty-eight hours, had cleared on 22 August, ostensibly for New York.

The source of this information was in part injudicious use of radio by the Germans and in part *Arlanza*. Her crew had managed to jury-rig a workable radio out of spare parts and as she entered the port at Las Palmas she was able to radio the armoured cruiser *Cornwall*. Clearly, cruiser warfare rules meant commerce raiders were putting themselves at risk in releasing enemy merchantmen and in reality it was hard to silence a radio-equipped ship without sinking it.

Buller was immediately informed and set off at once, finding the German ship under its plume of coal dust on 26 August. She was coaling between two ships off the coastline, with a third collier standing off. *Kaiser Wilhelm*'s boiler fires were damped down and although much the faster vessel in open sea, she was effectively trapped against the coastline. This therefore looked a very one-sided contest but for the complication of neutrality, for in contrast to *Highflyer*'s armament *Kaiser Wilhelm* mounted only smaller weapons for trade interdiction, six 10.5cm (about 4in) guns firing 38lb shells. Buller called on Reymann to surrender, to which the German captain replied, 'German warships do not surrender. I request you to observe Spanish neutrality,' and ran up the German ensign. This rather ignored the fact that Reymann was violating such neutrality himself and Buller signalled to that effect, adding for good measure that he would sink her if she refused to surrender immediately. This Reymann again refused to do, as he did once more when an hour later Buller repeated his threat, giving Reymann the option of striking his flag or putting out to sea.

Henry Buller, conscious of both the passage of time and the fact that valuable ships were tied up and kept from other duties by the German's mere presence in the area, took the bull by the horns. He was a Royal Navy captain. It was expected that he would take the offensive. He was also a man of considerable self-belief. Rarely has the Admiralty censured a captain for being over-aggressive. Buller decided that, neutrality or not, he was going to have a shooting match.

Highflyer manoeuvred to get a range clear of the land, and at 1500 fired the opening shot. The Germans at once returned fire and the unequal action began. At the same time, the German captain, with the chivalry for which he has already been noted, sent his 100 prisoners away on one of the colliers, *Arucas*, which had been moored to the liner's port side (they were later landed in the Canary Islands) and prepared for action. The other two colliers made off as best they could.

For an hour and a half both ships kept up a brisk fire, but at 1645 *Kaiser Wilhelm* ceased fire and boats were seen to be leaving her. The liner's portside forward gun had been shot away, one side of her bridge destroyed by gunfire, and she was on fire aft. Thinking to save further bloodshed, Captain Buller signalled her to haul down her flag and he sent off his own boats under the Red Cross flag with medical assistance. But before his boats could reach the battered ship, the German vessel turned over in the shallow water, lying on her beam and showing her starboard side uppermost. As the crew now ashore had taken up a menacing defensive position behind the sandhills, Buller recalled his boats and left the Germans to their own devices.

The German account later claimed that *Kaiser Wilhelm der Grosse* ran out of ammunition. According to their report, rather than let the enemy capture his ship, Reymann ordered her to be scuttled using dynamite, which was already in position. Detonated in the engine room and sixteen other compartments, the explosives tore a large hole in the vessel, causing her to capsize. A letter from an officer on *Kaiser Wilhelm der Grosse* to his mother was printed in the *Berliner Tageblatt* and reported in the British press: 'We fired off all our ammunition and then sank our dear *Kaiser Wilhelm der Grosse* and reached land in our small boats. The English shooting was painfully bad.'

This version of events was disputed by the British, who stated that the ship had been badly damaged and sinking when Reymann ordered it to be abandoned. The Admiralty firmly asserted that it was gunfire from *Highflyer* which sank the German liner.

Reymann himself managed to swim to shore, and made his way back to Germany by working as a stoker on a neutral vessel. Some of his crew marched off to the nearest Spanish fort, where they were rather surprised to find themselves handed over to British forces and sent for internment in Nova Scotia for the remainder of the war. The rest set sail in the tender *Bethania* and were captured at sea trying to reach America.

Highflyer was virtually unscathed and lost only one man killed (a carpenter), with five wounded, perhaps a function of the lack of training of the German gunners.

The Admiralty sent a congratulatory telegram to Captain Buller: 'Bravo! You have rendered a service not only to Britain but to the peaceful commerce of the world. The German officers and crew appear to have carried out their duties with humanity and restraint and are therefore worthy of seamanlike consideration.'

Naturally, the Spanish government complained of British violation of neutral waters; the diplomats replied that, as the *Kaiser Wilhelm* had used the harbour as a base for nine days and had apparently been met there by no less than four colliers and supply ships, there was no case to answer. The Spanish took the obvious course and, after admitting both sides were to blame and presenting an amicable but energetic protest to both Britain and Germany, let the matter drop.

Buller faced a perfunctory Admiralty inquiry which cleared him of any misdeeds. As the *Official History* stated much later:

> to have left the offending ship untouched would have been to invite hostile commerce destroyers to seek sanctuary in similar unfrequented [neutral] anchorages all over the world. A letter of apology in this vein was sent to the Spanish authorities, the apology was accepted, and, in spite of a vigorous German Press campaign in Spain, no more was heard of the affair.

Churchill had meanwhile been able to announce a British victory in the House of Commons. It was a much needed boost, for in the same week that *Kaiser Wilhelm* was destroyed, Louvain lay a smoking ruin, Sir John French and the British Expeditionary Force (BEF) were in a full-scale retreat and the Russian 'steamroller' had just been crushed in the swamps of Tannenberg.

4

Dancing Elephants, 1914

The liner *Cap Trafalgar* had been built for the famous German shipping company Hamburg Sud-Amerika for service between Hamburg and the River Plate. She could carry 1,600 passengers in some style and made her maiden voyage on 19 April 1914. At 613ft and 18,710grt she was the largest and most luxurious ship yet built for the company. She was also earmarked by the Imperial German Navy for service as a *Hilfskreuzer*.

When war was declared in Europe in August, *Cap Trafalgar* was in Buenos Aires, laid up pending orders. She was immediately requisitioned for the Kaiserliche Marine as an AMC by the German attaché in Buenos Aires and set sail for Montevideo for coaling, arriving on 18 August. From there she made her way to the remote Brazilian island of Trinidada, five hundred miles east of the Brazilian mainland, where the gunboat SMS *Eber* (of the German West African Squadron) rendezvoused with her and transferred naval officers (including her new captain, Korvettenkapitän [Lieutenant Commander] Julius Wirth, thirty-nine years old, who had been in command of the gunboat until transferring to the AMC), ammunition and armaments to the liner. At the same time she adopted the disguise of a British liner believed to be in the area, *Carmania*. Now named SMS *Cap Trafalgar* (and given the codename *Hilfskreuzer B*), she set out on her mission to destroy British trade in the southern Atlantic. It was not a fruitful adventure and she returned to her supply base at Trinidada on 13 September to take on fuel from German colliers.

The British, too, were anxious to disrupt German trade from South America, particularly that of nitrates from Chile, which were essential to the manufacture of ammonia, a key chemical in explosives production, and to protect their own commerce, particularly foodstuffs. They too had supplemented their cruiser forces with AMCs.

The Cunard liner *Carmania* had been requisitioned by the navy eleven days after the outbreak of war. She was huge: 19,600grt and 650ft. When launched in 1905, *Carmania* and her running mate, *Caronia* (known as the 'Pretty Sisters') were the largest ships in the Cunard fleet and two of the fastest in the world, deliberately so, as they had been designed to compete with the Germans for the Blue Riband. Fitted out with an armament of eight naval guns, she sailed from Liverpool and arrived at Shell Bay, Bermuda, on 23 August. In command was a full navy captain, Noel Grant, whilst her captain in pre-war times, Captain James Barr, was appointed as her second in command with the rank of commander RNR (Royal Naval Reserve).

Grant was an experienced commander. Born in 1868 he had joined the navy twelve years later and achieved the rank of captain at the end of 1908. His appointments had included captain of the second-class cruiser *Leander*, a spell as captain (D) in command of the 5th Destroyer Flotilla and captain of the pre-dreadnought battleship *Irresistible*. He was nobody's fool.

At Bermuda, Grant was informed that *Cap Trafalgar* and two smaller ships had been reported as being sighted off the Brazilian coast. He hardly needed the orders he received to set out and find her. Thus it was that, attracted by the dust given off by *Cap Trafalgar*'s coaling, Grant took *Carmania* towards Trinidada and to the first ever battle between two AMCs.

Both ships were bigger than most contemporary battleships. *Dreadnought*, the mighty ship that had revolutionised naval construction and strategy, measured less in length and was equal in gross tonnage (527ft, 20,000 tons), and the Royal Navy's magnificent *Queen Elizabeth*-class battleships, just coming into service, were only a little larger (645ft and 27,500 tons).

The Germans had armed *Cap Trafalgar* with two 4.1in guns and six 1pdr pom-poms, all manned by experienced naval personnel;

this was an armament suitable for the interception and destruction of merchant ships, but not one that gave it much hitting power against other classes of vessel. The 4.1in guns threw a shell of 38lbs weight to a range of 13,900yds. The pom-poms were intended only for close engagements, firing a 1lb shell at a maximum range of 4,500yds. By contrast, *Carmania* was equipped with eight 4.7in guns, arranged to fire a broadside of four at any time, discharging a 45lb shell to a distance of 10,000–12,000yds when new, but they were old and worn and the maximum range was now less than 9,000yds.

Both captains realised that to fight a successful action their enormous vessels required plenty of room, and they had separately steamed several miles away from the little island in order to gain the space required. The German ship also sent out encoded messages, announcing the engagement with *Carmania,* and gave their position as 35° W, 26° S, with a heading of NNW.

Once with sufficient sea room, the two ships turned towards each other and at 1100 began to fight, *Carmania* firing when out of range and thus allowing *Cap Trafalgar* the first success. *Carmania* suffered much the worse of the engagement in the following two hours, being hit seventy-nine times, holed at the waterline, and having her bridge totally destroyed by shellfire. Lieutenant Murchie RNR, commanding No 1 gun in the starboard battery, lost practically the whole of his gun crew from a direct hit, but with the aid of one remaining gunner continued to keep the gun in action. Grant had meantime abandoned the forebridge, and conned the ship from aft using the lower steering position.

Wirth was desperate to close the range so that he could bring his pom-poms into action. With his limited armament he concentrated on the command bridge, in the hope of decapitating *Carmania's* command structure, whilst Captain Grant, with his superior fire-power, concentrated on the waterline of his opponent, a strategy which, although sensible, allowed his opponent to fight his guns without fear of counter-fire. However, as the range closed, *Carmania's* heavier armament began to take a toll and fires took hold on both ships. The big British liner's fire main had been shot through and chemical fire extinguishers to which the fire crews reverted proved to be useless. Sailors took to lining the rails and firing machine guns at their opposite numbers as the ships came within a few hundred yards of each other, in a manner of fighting that would have been familiar to Nelson or Jervis, and Grant was able to circle round the German ship and pour constant fire into her.

An eyewitness on board the British ship, Wireless Operator Arnold Rushforth, described the scene:

> I could not explain my feelings during our fierce fight but I know I thought of you as the shot and shell were flying all around and above me. I expected every moment to be my last but my time was not yet come. I had many narrow escapes and in memory of that never-to-be-forgotten event I have got a few pieces of German shells which I picked off the deck and am bringing home.
>
> Our brave captain was as cool as ninepence. He drove the *Carmania* at full speed during the whole conflict and circled round the German ship at such sharp angles that I thought once we were sinking so badly did our ship heel over.
>
> As the saying was at the time 'We gave the Germans hell.' Our gunners fought up to the old reputation of the bulldog breed. Every man fought with never-tiring energy and their marksmanship was splendid. They rattled the shells in one after the other and got home about four shells to the Germans' one.

The fires on *Carmania*'s bridge caused her to turn away full circle until she was chasing, but the German was also on fire forward with a slight list. As a stern chase developed, *Cap Trafalgar* slowly pulled away but with fires gaining and her list increasing. Grant was worried; the fires on his ship were also burning fiercely and his enemy seemed to be getting away. But then *Cap Trafalgar* veered away, lowering lifeboats as she heeled over to port. A shell below the waterline had ruptured several compartments, and the ship was rapidly sinking. Her listing was such that many of her boats could not be launched. Mortally wounded, she broke off the engagement and limped back towards Trinidada. In compliance with the Kaiser's standing orders, Wirth commanded that the seacocks be opened and explosives set off in her engine room. At 1330 she rolled over and sank in position 20° 10′ S, 29° 51′ W, taking seventeen crew with her, including her captain who had been severely wounded during the action.

Because of the heavy and accurate fire, and the disguise Wirth had affected (he had, by a strange irony, attempted to represent his ship as *Carmania*), Captain Grant was uncertain which ship he had sunk and, in any case, believed it to be more heavily armed than it had been. But if Grant thought that his troubles were over at this point he would have been wrong. *Carmania* was badly damaged, listing severely, heavily flooded and on fire, with many men dead and wounded. And now a new ship appeared on the horizon, the armed merchant cruiser *Kronprinz Wilhelm*. Grant's ship was in no condition to fight a new opponent but, in an act that might in the Royal Navy have resulted in a court martial, *Kronprinz Wilhelm*'s captain turned away, presumably fearing a trap, on the basis that other warships must have heard the radio signals of both combatants if he had. Grant and his crew were safe, although with a badly damaged ship to nurse to safety. *Carmania* had five holes on the waterline and her navigating bridge was destroyed.

Wireless Operator Rushforth noted: 'Our ship however looks a sorry sight for it is almost full of shell holes and the captain's bridge and officers' quarters were completely burnt out (the ship got on fire during the fight). Though the enemy fought well, our boys fought better and they deserve great praise for the victory over the *Cap Trafalgar*.'

Getting the fires under control, *Carmania* limped towards the coaling station of Abrolhos Rocks, where next afternoon she was met by the old cruiser *Bristol*, which stood by until the arrival of the armoured cruiser *Cornwall*. She had lost six men killed (with a further four who died of their wounds later) and had twenty-six wounded sailors on board. Of the ten who died, seven were Royal Naval Reserve (RNR), one Royal Navy, one a Marine and one Merchant Marine Reserve.

As for the Germans, their colliers rescued close on three hundred men who were taken ashore in Argentina where they were interned for the duration of the war. The crew of *Eber* sought refuge in Bahia where they and their ship were also interned by the Brazilians.

Of the three German AMCs loose in the Atlantic, two had now been dealt with. Two massive ships had fought a battle they were never designed for and the Royal Navy had emerged victorious.

First Lord Winston Churchill was quick to praise the action, sending Grant a congratulatory telegram: 'Well done! You have fought a fine action to a successful finish.' And the *Daily Telegraph* (which incorrectly claimed the enemy was armed with eight 4in guns and which identified it as *Cap Trafalgar* or *Berlin*) noted 'there is one German marauder less on the high sea'.

Noel Grant and James Barr both received the CB for the action and there were further awards of a DSO, three DSCs and twelve DSMs to the ship's company. Grant was also honoured by a stamp! The Lord Roberts Memorial Fund for disabled soldiers and sailors, which flourished between 1915 and 1917, issued a series of 144 stamps to raise money for the fund; Captain Noel Grant CB featured on one of them.

There was an interesting postscript to the tale. On the arrival in Argentina of the German survivors, the Uruguayan authorities – at the request of a scheming British embassy in Uruguay, who stated that the German liner had concealed her weaponry from them when in the neutral harbour of Montevideo – asked for, and received, the extradition of the liner's original captain, Langerhannsz, for trial. His testimony was presented to the court by his lawyer and sent to Grant for comment. Embarrassed that he had suffered so much damage at the hands of such an outgunned foe, Grant never replied and Langerhannsz's testimony went unchallenged. He was released into internment.

5

The Weary Traveller, 1914–1915

Churchill had predicted that at the start of the war there would be forty or so German civilian passenger vessels lying in eastern continental American ports waiting to prey on British shipping. In fact, only three big liners managed a successful transformation to AMC, the third being *Kronprinz Wilhelm*.

She was another NDL ship, sister to *Kaiser Wilhelm der Grosse*, and of similar size and proportions, 663ft and displacing 24,900 tons. Like her sister, she had held the Blue Riband for an Atlantic crossing from Cherbourg to New York in a time of five days, eleven hours, fifty-seven minutes, with an average speed of 23.09 knots, completed in September 1902. The role she was now about to fill had been preordained for her since 1901, when she was built with a strong design input from the Imperial German Navy regarding the number of watertight compartments fitted to improve her abilities to withstand attack.

On 4 August, when the declaration of war between Britain and Germany became effective, she was in port at Hoboken, New Jersey, having arrived in the USA ten days beforehand from Bremerhaven under Captain Grahn. The NDL line immediately cancelled all future bookings and Grahn set sail, saying that he was leaving for home. It was common knowledge, however, that she had been loaded to the gunnels with coal, which had been stored in every conceivable space, including the elaborate and ornate grand saloon.

Rather than Germany, her destination was the sea between the Florida coast and Bermuda, and there she rendezvoused with the German light cruiser *Karlsruhe*. From the cruiser she obtained two

3.46in (88mm) rapid-firing guns, 290 rounds of 88mm ammunition, a machine gun, and thirty-six rifles, as well as one officer, two non-commissioned officers, and thirteen ratings. Kapitanleutnant Paul Wolfgang Thierfelder, who had been serving as *Karlsruhe*'s navigator, took over the captaincy and Grahn became his first officer and second in command.

The meeting of the two raiders was, however, truncated by the untimely report of the close proximity of the British cruiser *Suffolk*, under the command of Rear Admiral Sir Christopher Cradock, who was hunting for *Karlsruhe* with the 4th Cruiser Squadron from his base in Bermuda. The Germans made a hasty escape and Cradock chased *Karlsruhe*, whose superior speed over the antiquated British cruiser allowed her to avoid being brought to action. Thierfelder, meanwhile, took his new command to the Azores by a deliberately meandering route (forced on him as his armament had not yet been properly installed and he could not risk meeting enemy ships), where he was able to complete his provisioning and arming from the German steamer *Walhalla* on 17 August, off São Miguel Island. He also took on coal, but discovered that there would be no more available to him from Spanish neutral territory and decided instead to head for the coast of Brazil.

Now began a remarkable cruise. During the next eight months, *Kronprinz Wilhelm* cruised the waters off the coast of Brazil and Argentina. Allied newspapers often reported her sunk, torpedoed, or interned, but fallaciously, for between 4 September 1914 and 28 March 1915 she was responsible for the capture (and generally the subsequent sinking) of fifteen ships – ten British, four French and one Norwegian – off the east coast of South America. Thirteen of them were sunk by the direct actions of *Kronprinz Wilhelm*; another she damaged severely by ramming, leading to its later loss. The remaining vessel was used after her twelfth capture to transport into port what had become an unbearable number of detainees imprisoned on board. Her victims totalled over 57,000 tons of Allied shipping and caused much naval resource to be devoted to seemingly futile task of finding her, as well as disrupting the South American trade routes to the UK.

Her captain's methods were simple. Ships were captured either by *Kronprinz Wilhelm* overtaking them with superior speed, ordering them to stop and then sending over a boarding party; or by pretending to be a ship in distress (or of a friendly nationality) and luring unsuspecting prey to her by subterfuge. Her victims were sailing singly, not designed to put up a fight and a long way from any possible assistance. Their captains had thus to make a rapid decision of whether to run, fight or surrender. Given that their ships were no match in speed and usually had little or no armament, the unpleasant but safe choice was surrender. Thierfelder would send over a boarding party to search the captured vessel. If it found nothing of value or military significance, the ship was released and sent on its way. If valuable cargo, and especially coal, was discovered, or the vessel was judged to be one that might someday be converted to military use, the crew of *Kronprinz Wilhelm* would systematically and (apparently) politely transfer all of the crew, passengers, their baggage and other useful cargo from the captured ship, which was then scuttled by opening up the seacocks* and detonating explosive charges. Remarkably, throughout the entire cruise, not a single life was lost either by the crew themselves or their prisoners.

Thierfelder's ability to maintain his ship at sea depended first on him getting regular supplies of coal (the need for which had helped drive the other two large liners to their end), and secondly, on his position remaining unreported, for in any shooting match with a naval vessel his minor armament would be of limited use. Fortunately for him, German agents in a variety of South American countries were able to procure coal and arrange for colliers to meet with him to tranship it. From leaving Hoboken, in her whole cruise *Kronprinz* did not put into port.

But the huge vessel's need for constant replenishment was her Achilles' heel. Coal was always a worry and so were fresh foodstuffs. Diet deteriorated over time and with it the health of the crew. Scurvy – the curse of sailors down the centuries – broke out and thus minor injuries refused to heal, haemorrhaging was commonplace and lassitude often took hold. It might be noted that these were the

---

*A seacock is a valve (often a Kingston valve) on the hull of a boat or a ship, permitting water to flow into the vessel – such as for cooling an engine or for a salt water tap – or out of the boat, such as for a sink drain or a toilet. Opening the seacocks (and then leaving them open) is one of the main methods used to scuttle a ship so that it cannot be captured by the enemy.

travails of the lower deck. Whatever fresh vegetables and fruit could been obtained from her prizes was reserved for the officers' mess!

The end came in March 1915. Thierfelder had headed north to rendezvous with another German supply ship near the equator. He arrived at the meeting point on the morning of 28 March and cruised in the neighbourhood all day without making contact. *Kronprinz Wilhelm* steamed round the area for several days without success; and with good reason for the supply ship, *Macedonia*, had been captured by British warships on the day of the intended rendezvous and escorted to port.

Short of coal and with the health of his crew now in rapid decline, Thierfelder reluctantly made his decision. Early on the morning of 11 April, *Kronprinz Wilhelm* hove to near Cape Henry, Virginia, and took on board a pilot. At 1012 that morning she dropped anchor off Newport News. For the ship and her crew, it meant internment for the remaining duration of the war.

In a remarkable cruise, the ship had steamed 32,731 nautical miles without once being detected or putting into a harbour. Thierfelder's caution had had a downside, for he missed the chance to finish off *Carmania*, as noted in the previous chapter. But it was a considerable achievement, and shows what might have happened if more of Germany's large fast liners had got past the British blockade, or had been pre-positioned with sufficient coal supply by a German Admiralty caught flat-footed by the declaration of war.

*   *   *

The demise of the three big German passenger liners was not the whole story of the Imperial Navy's first attempts at disrupting Britain's supply lines through cruiser warfare.

The Imperial Navy converted other liners with minimal success, bar one. The passenger ship *Berlin* (26,000 tons) was commissioned as *Hilfskreuzer C* in September 1914. It was first planned to send the ship into the Atlantic, but its slow speed led to this objective being abandoned as impractical. Instead, the ship was used to lay a minefield off Glasgow and then attack merchant shipping in the Barents Sea. Like so many of her sisters, she was badly impacted by her huge coal consumption and sailed to Trondheim for sanctuary when short of fuel and was interned on 18 November.

Prinz Eitel Friedrich was a liner of 16,000 tons and was positioned in southeast Asia when the First World War broke out. After being equipped as an auxiliary cruiser at the German East Asiatic squadron base of Tsingtau in China, she first served as flagship for all auxiliary vessels there. After that she operated with Vice Admiral Graf von Spee's cruisers (*vide infra*) off the South American coast for a short time and then set off on her own merchant warfare operation in October 1914. In the following seven months, she sank or captured eleven ships in the Pacific and the South Atlantic. Once again, after this limited success, coal shortages supervened and she sailed into Newport News, USA, for internment on 9 April 1915.

The former Russian passenger steamer *Riäsan* (7,250 tons) was captured by SMS *Emden* on 4 September 1914. Sent to Tsingtau, the ship was renamed *Cormoran* and equipped with the guns of an old gunboat of the same name. Despatched to operate in the South Pacific, she met with no success. Eventually, because of coal shortages, she sailed to the American neutral port of Guam, where she was interned. When the USA entered the war in 1917, the ship was scuttled by her crew on 7 April 1917, after a firefight with American troops intent on her capture.

Cap Polonio, a liner of 24,500 tons, was modified to an auxiliary cruiser and renamed *Vienta* in early 1915. Although a brand-new ship, in her trials it proved impossible to attain her designed top speed of 17 knots, which made her too slow for her intended role and she was de-armed and returned to port.

The German fast liner auxiliary cruisers had proved too recognisable, large and fuel-inefficient for their task. The British Empire had required the acquisition of major coaling bases on all the key trade routes of the world. Thus the British navy was never very far from a source of succour. The Germans, who despite feeling they should have an empire had failed to acquire much of one and had few naval bases to support it, had no such access to coal. It was the downfall of their first attempt at cruiser warfare.

And then there were the activities of the regular German Imperial Navy cruisers, which were essentially confined to the voyages of the East Asiatic Squadron under Admiral von Spee.

They had been forced to abandon their base of Tsingtau by

advancing Japanese forces and von Spee was attempting to make his way back to Germany via the Pacific and Atlantic oceans whilst also on the lookout for the opportunity to damage British interests when he could. He detached the light cruiser *Emden* for trade interdiction in the waters around India, and *Emden*, under her enterprising captain, Karl von Müller, made the most of the opportunity.

In the Indian Ocean the German cruiser sank 70,825 gross tons of Allied shipping, including warships, between August and October 1914, and paralysed trade in and around the major Indian trade and supply routes. In all instances she obeyed the 'rules' of cruiser warfare and, indeed, her captain gained a considerable reputation for chivalry and courtesy. No one seemed able to catch her until she was run to ground by HMAS *Sydney* and sunk.

As an example of the disruption a determined commerce raider can make, *Emden*'s example was instructive. All told, she sank two Allied warships and captured thirty merchant vessels. Trade was virtually shut down as owners panicked and the vital Singapore–Colombo route stopped running. *Emden* had, single-handedly, brought shipping to a key part of the empire to a halt, and the Admiralty were terrified that von Spee and his ships could do the same to the critical North Atlantic trade routes if they got there.

However, their dispositions were at best flawed and at worst criminal, not assisted by Churchill's daily interference. Von Spee was able to destroy Rear Admiral 'Kit' Cradock's 4th Cruiser Squadron in a one-sided engagement off Coronel, on the Chilean coast, in which the admiral and over 1,600 British sailors died bravely but futilely, before von Spee met his own death at the hands of Admiral Sturdee's avenging squadron of battlecruisers on 8 December 1914.

With the internment of *Kronprinz Wilhelm* just three months later, the German surface raider threat was removed from the oceans. They would have to find another answer.

6

Enter the U-boat, 1914–1916

Following the collapse of the first phases of Germany's commerce war, the Imperial German Navy turned to the U-boat arm as an alternative. Large, fast passenger liners had been seen as ideal weapons in the trade war, but their sheer size in fact worked against them. Heavy coal consumption, of large profile, and possessed of no armour at all, they were found wanting. U-boats did not suffer from these disadvantages, but had others all of their own in the conduct of cruiser warfare under prize rules.

Despite some successes, the inadequacies of the U-boat as a commerce raider quickly became apparent. Lacking the speed and gun armament of an AMC with which to entrap, overawe or overpower its victims, U-boats were increasingly faced with ships that would resist capture by running faster than they could, or, as more and more became defensively armed, by shooting back.

Fisher himself had stated, 'there is nothing a submarine can do except sink her capture' (see Chapter 2), and under the internationally agreed prize rules of cruiser warfare this was anathema.

Warships, however, were a different kettle of fish altogether and the German submarine navy set about its British opponent with a will. To HMS *Pathfinder*, a scout cruiser launched in 1904, went the doubtful distinction of becoming the first Royal Naval vessel to be sunk by a locomotive torpedo when, on 5 September, she was torpedoed off St Abb's Head, near Berwick. As a result of one of the many faults of this misbegotten class – that of limited coal storage and hence poor endurance – she was proceeding at only 5 knots due to a shortage of fuel, and presented an easy target. At 1550 a torpedo detonated beneath the bridge. This set off a fire in some cordite charges, leading to a flash which caused a devastating explosion within the fore section of the ship as the magazine blew up. The fore mast and No 1 funnel collapsed and then toppled over the side, and the whole of the forward part of the ship was destroyed, all this in broad daylight and in full view of land.

Out of a crew of 270, just eighteen people survived. Captain F M Leake, was, as tradition enjoined, the last to leave his rapidly sinking ship, having called out to his crew, 'Jump you devils, jump!' Leake later wrote to his mother:

It was Saturday afternoon at 3.45, we had sent the TBDs off on various errands and were returning from a sweep out to sea to investigate shipping, etc. I had just left the bridge and was in my after cabin standing by the table when the screws began to stop. I started a bolt to see what it was, but before I got away from the table, she gave a veritable stagger and tremble and everything movable came tumbling down. I got up the ladder, pushed the hatch cover up (it had come down), then got the boy (my valet) out, and had a look round.

Every sort of thing was in the air. Shell room forward seemed still to be going up. The torpedo got us in our forward magazine and evidently sent this up, thereby killing everyone forward. Her upper deck was flush with the water forward and it was only a question of how long she would float. Both our cutters were smashed up, the whaler was whole so all that could be done was to get this boat out and throw all floatable matter over. A badly hurt man was brought aft and put on the QD. While this was going on she began decidedly to go down by the bows and the 1st lieutenant gave the order for jumping overboard, he judged this very well. Personally I stayed too long and found myself on the after shelter deck with the ship rapidly assuming an upright position. I decided to stand on the searchlight stand and take my chance. This soon went under and self as well, come up again, ship still there, had another dive and then got shot right clear. The situation then developed, an oar came along and then a blue jacket. Then another oar and another blue jacket. Looked for ship, found her still on her nose (probably on the bottom) she then fell over and disappeared, leaving a mass of wreckage all round, but I regret a very few men amongst it, for at the time they were all asleep on the mess decks and the full explosion must have caught them, for no survivors came from forward. I found one of the sailors with me had a broken leg. This prevented propelling our oars to where more wood was. So I swam away to a more plentiful supply, and met a meat safe, I knocked the end out of this and was busy at the other end when I snuffed out for a time.

Leake had, in fact, badly cut his head and nearly bled to death. A torpedo boat pulled him out of the water and he survived. We shall meet him again later. Other survivors were rescued by the St Abb's lifeboat, *Helen Smitton*. When she put into harbour, Aldous Huxley reported in a letter to his father of 14 September that 'there was not a piece of wood, they said, big enough to float a man – and over acres the sea was covered with fragments – human and otherwise. They brought back a sailor's cap with half a man's head inside it. The explosion must have been frightful.'

The Admiralty, unwilling to admit that it was a submarine victory, announced that the vessel had hit a mine and, when that was exposed as a fallacy, that the submarine concerned had been cornered by cruisers and shelled to death. Neither point was true. Both the submarine concerned (*U-21*) and the German commander, Otto Hersing, survived the war.

Then, on 22 September, three old armoured cruisers were patrolling off the Dutch coast. They had been, as Battenberg (First Sea Lord at the time) put it, 'peddling up and down' here since the outbreak of war, to keep an eye on possible German light craft activity. They were elderly, vulnerable and predictable. Officially called Force C, they were known in the navy as 'the live bait squadron'. At 0630 *Aboukir* was hit by a torpedo and sank. *Hogue* was trying to rescue survivors when she too was hit and sank in ten minutes. *Cressy,* which by now should have been running for her life, unbelievably hove to and at 0717 capsized, having been hit by two torpedoes. All three ships had been sunk by one submarine, *U-9*, commanded by Kapitänleutnant Otto Weddigen. Sixty-two officers and 1,397 men (mostly middle-aged reservists and cadets straight out of the Dartmouth naval college) went down with the ships – ships which were of little or no value, but the men were.

Three weeks later, on 15 October, *U-9*, once again on patrol in the North Sea, torpedoed the ancient cruiser *Hawke*, resulting in the death of 524 men. Then on 31 October *Hermes*, a seaplane carrier, was torpedoed by *U-27* whilst cruising in the Straits of Dover and sank with the loss of twenty-two crew. *Niger*, a converted minesweeper, was sunk by *U-12* in the roadstead of the Downs (off the coast of Deal in Kent) on 11 November, fortunately with only one crew member lost.

And on New Year's Day 1915, in appalling weather, the British battleship *Formidable* was sunk by Kapitänleutnant Rudolph Schneider in *U-24* with appalling loss of life. Only twenty miles from the Dorset coast, nearly six hundred men and boys perished.

Clearly, those who had dismissed the submarine as a weapon of war, called it a 'toy', or misread its capabilities in open water, were wrong. When not constrained by the rules of cruiser warfare, the submarine was a potent weapon of destruction.

*   *   *

On 20 October 1914 the 866-ton British steamer *Glitra*, proceeding off the coast of Norway, became the first merchantman ever to be sunk by a submarine. The German commander, Kapitanleutnant Feldkirchner in *U-17* conducted the affair under cruiser warfare rules. Operating on the surface, he hailed the ship and ordered her to heave to, sending over a boarding party. *Glitra*'s crew were given ten minutes to take to their boats and, after 'giving an exhibition of hatred for the British flag', the little ship's seacocks were opened and she sank without loss of life. It was all very correct – and slow, laborious, and dangerous to the submarine.

In the first six months of the war, the entire German submarine effort sank only ten merchantmen totalling 20,000 tons; less than *Emden* or *Kronprinz*. All were sunk according to the rules and usually without the use of torpedoes.

Their lack of success was not due to any avoidance of sea-time. Whilst the German battlefleet hid in the Elbe and Jade, submarines were regularly on patrol. Indeed it was the submarine branch of the

Kaiserliche Marine which discovered that the expected close blockade was not being applied by Britain.

But, disappointed by the performance of their AMCs and the loss of von Spee's cruiser squadron, and annoyed that the insistence on following the 'rules' of commerce warfare made their remaining weapon – the U-boat – ineffective, the German High Command pressed for an unrestricted submarine campaign against all Allied shipping. Their wish was granted on 4 February 1915 when Germany declared a war zone around the British Isles in which ships would be sunk without warning. Neutrals were also told that their shipping was equally at risk.

In this decision lay the kernel of a problem, for the German establishment was keen to avoid antagonising neutrals such as Italy and America, in an attempt to keep them out of the war. Thus it was that when on 7 May *U-20* torpedoed SS *Lusitania*, an unarmed liner on the Atlantic run, with the loss of 1,198 passengers and crew – including 128 Americans – the protests of the US government gave some cause for concern in Berlin. President Woodrow Wilson condemned the killing of Americans stating, 'no warning that an unlawful and inhumane act will be committed can possibly be accepted as an excuse of palliation'. Anti-German rioting broke out in American and British cities, with property worth over £40,000 destroyed in Liverpool alone.

However, these protests did not manifest themselves in any change of strategy and the Germans justified the *Lusitania* and other sinkings as reprisals for the British blockade of the German coast, which was causing severe food shortages. Next, the liner *Arabic* was sunk off the coast of Ireland by *U-24* with heavy loss of life, including three Americans, on 19 August. This time the American diplomatic protest was so sharp that the imperial government felt constrained to act and the German navy was prohibited from attacking liners of any nationality without giving due warning and ensuring the safety of passengers. As this would have exposed the submarines to considerable risk, the decision was taken to withdraw them from western waters altogether.

Still fixated by the issue of potential American intervention, the Germans announced a new campaign on 11 February 1916, in which only enemy merchantmen within the war zone would be considered as fair game; outside, they could only be sunk without the application of international rules, and armed and passenger liners were not to be interfered with in any way.

Nonetheless, on 24 March *U(B)-29* torpedoed and sank the French passenger steamer *Sussex*, crossing between Dieppe and Folkestone. She was carrying 380 souls, including American citizens, some of whom perished or were injured. This time the US government's protests were unequivocal. Germany must cease and desist immediately or face the consequences. The imperial regime was so alarmed that it instructed its naval staff to prohibit all attacks outside prize rules. Angry and frustrated, on 24 April Admiral von Scheer ordered his U-boats to port. Trade flowed freely again. Once more German commerce raiding had failed. What could be done?

7
The Seagull, 1915–1917

Like Britain, Germany relied heavily on imports for both her industrial complex and to feed her population. By 1915 it was becoming clear that the blockading activities of the Royal Navy were having a considerable impact on both of these requirements. German imports had fallen by 55 per cent from pre-war levels. Aside from causing shortages in important raw materials such as coal and various non-ferrous metals, the blockade cut off fertiliser supplies which were vital to German agriculture. Food rationing had been introduced in January 1915 and the restrictions tightened throughout the year. But, with the withdrawal of her submarines from western waters in August and the failure of her armed liners project, Germany was unable to seriously interdict British trade (Britain would not, in fact, introduce rationing until 1918).

There was public unrest in Germany at this, from a Teutonic perspective, inequitable situation. Something needed to be done. But what?

In October 1915 a relatively junior officer, Leutnant zur See Theodor Wolff, wrote a paper in which he suggested that the navy should look to the use of anonymous and commonplace freighters, fit them out with extra coal bunkerage to increase their range, and arm them. If ships could be chosen that had sufficient speed to overtake the relatively slow British tramp steamers which formed the core of the British merchant marine, then their success as raiders should be assured; and the fact that they looked just like any other of such cargo ships tramping the oceans of the world would make it difficult for blockading and searching ships to spot them. Wolff did not, however, live to see his plan through, drowning when he was washed overboard from a U-boat.

Admiral Pohl, the German commander-in-chief, still fuming over the decision imposed on him regarding withdrawing his U-boats, was persuaded to try out this concept of the Armed Merchant Ship once more.

As his instrument he chose a Silesian aristocrat, Korvettenkapitan Nikolaus Burggraf und Graf zu Dohna-Schlodien, who was ordered to seek out a suitable ship for fitting out, initially as a minelayer.

Dohna-Schlodien was a career sailor who had joined the Imperial Navy in 1896 at the age of seventeen and made second lieutenant three years later and first lieutenant in 1902. He fought in the Boxer rebellion, immediately afterwards served on *Tiger* in East Asia for two years, and was commander of the gunboat *Tsingtau* in 1910–1912. In 1913 he was appointed navigation officer of the battleship *Posen* and was promoted to Korvettenkapitän. Dark, with alert eyes and a pointed beard, he had a piratical mien. But he had another characteristic more valuable than his service record would suggest. He was a maverick. And he saw in Wolff's plan the opportunity for the next generation of commerce raiders.

He needed a ship that looked ordinary, was strong enough to carry a heavy armament, and fast enough to have a speed advantage over his prey. And Dohna-Schlodien found it in a banana carrier, bottled up in Bremen by the British blockade. She had been launched as the freighter *Pungo* in 1914 and operated by the Afrikanische Fruchtkompanie out of Hamburg, who employed her in an uneventful career carrying cargoes of bananas from the colony of Kamerun (today's Republic of Cameroon) to Germany. She was fast, strong and roomy. Dohna-Schlodien requisitioned her for the navy and sent her to Wilhelmshaven for conversion. Officially known as *HD 10*, or *Hilfsdampter 10* (Auxiliary Steamer 10), Dohna-Schlodien renamed her *Moewe*, German for 'seagull'.

When she emerged from the shipyard on 1 November 1915, she was a significant weapon. Armed with four 15cm guns forward (taken from a decommissioned battleship) and one 10.5cm gun aft, she mounted four side-launched torpedo tubes and carried 500 mines. All of her weapons were concealed by false hatches, deckhouses, etc, and her armament (roughly equivalent to four 6in and one 4in British naval guns) made her of greater firepower than anything she was likely to encounter up to a first-class cruiser.

Dohna-Schlodien took command of his new 13-knot ship and 235-man crew, ran a shakedown cruise and set to work. He and his ship were to prove the most successful surface commerce raider in the war.

Altogether, *Moewe* made three cruises. On 26 December 1915, escorted by the submarine *U-69*, *Moewe* slipped out of Wilhelmshaven on her first mission, which was to lay a minefield in the Pentland Firth, near the main base of the British Home Fleet at Scapa Flow. The weather was dreadful (running a force 8 gale) which helped her evade the Northern Blockade, as did her disguise, painted on in harbour and again at sea, hiding her golden funnel and white superstructure with the drab black of a tramp steamer and pretending to be the ship *Segoland* out of Gothenburg.

Despite the severe weather she successfully laid a field of 250 mines. A few days later the pre-dreadnought battleship *King Edward VII*, on her way to a refit in Belfast, struck one and, despite attempts to tow her to safety, sank. All but one of her 777-man crew was rescued. Dohna-Schlodien's orders now took him to the west coast of Ireland and to France. There he laid another minefield off the Gironde estuary, which sank a further two ships.

This mining part of her mission complete, *Moewe* moved into the Atlantic, operating first between Spain and the Canary Islands, and later off the coast of Brazil. Over the next few weeks she sank or captured fifteen cargo ships. Her modus operandi was to fly a red ensign, pretending to be British, or a neutral flag; using her superior speed she would overall her prize, demand it to heave to, transfer the crew and sink the victim by gunfire or, very occasionally, torpedo. On 15 January *Moewe* captured *Appam* which was carrying, apart from cargo, some German nationals destined for internment, the governor of Sierra Leone and the Nigerian administrator. Dohna-Schlodien solved a growing accommodation problem by transferring to her his 157 prisoners of war and sending them to neutral America. *Westburn*, taken on 8 February, served the same purpose.

Only once did *Moewe's* prey fight back. On 16 January she encountered *Clan Mactavish*, a 5,816-ton cargo boat returned from New Zealand. The British ship refused to stop and *Moewe* opened fire. A single gun mounted on the stern of *Clan Mactavish* replied, but the unequal contest was soon all over and eighteen British crew members were killed, with another five wounded. The Clan Line ship had sent out distress signals, which made Dohna-Schlodien extremely nervous but, despite the distress signals from *Clan Mactavish* being intercepted and read in the wireless room of the cruiser *Essex,* the telegraphist taking this message did not pass it on to his superiors. *Essex* was only 120 miles to the south, and another cruiser, *King Alfred,* was about the same distance to the north. Luck was definitely on the Germans' side. On 5 March she once more slipped through the blockade and entered harbour at Wilhelmshaven. For a Germany suffering food shortages and lacking in good news, her return was a propaganda triumph.

Bands played 'Deutschland über alles' as *Moewe* entered harbour. Two Imperial Navy cruisers hoisted all flags, to which *Moewe* replied with a hoist of the flags of the ships she had captured. A wireless message from the Kaiser greeted her captain. It read:

> I present to you and your gallant crew my most cordial greetings on the occasion of your return to a German port after your long and brilliantly successful cruise, and I offer my thanks for your heroism which has struck so vital a chord with all the German people. I confer on all your crew, the Iron Cross Second Class and I desire that you personally present yourself as soon as possible at Imperial Headquarters. Wilhelm IR.

Dohna-Schlodien travelled to Berlin by train and was presented at court, where he spent two hours with the Kaiser and was invested with Germany's highest award for bravery, the Pour le Mérite. He also gained the distinction of the casting of a special commemorative medal in recognition of his deeds and safe return. Designed by the artist M Gotze, and published by the Ball Company of Berlin, it depicted a bust of him in uniform and cap with, on the reverse, a nude man standing on the shore with arms outstretched, while a seagull flies over the partial port broadside view of a ship, inscribed above 'SMS MOEWE'. In a war of attrition he had become a beacon of hope.

After a short refit, *Moewe* set off on her second cruise, but this proved to be anti-climactic. In an effort to maintain security, she was renamed *Vineta,* after another auxiliary cruiser which had been withdrawn from service, and engaged in a series of short cruises during the summer of 1916 to attack Allied shipping off the coast of Norway. However, the magic touch had deserted her captain and this cruise only brought one success before she was ordered back to port for another refit prior to venturing once more into the Atlantic.

On 23 November *Moewe* set sail on her third cruise, which brought even more success than her first foray into the Atlantic. Disguised as a Swedish steamship, she slipped into the North Sea, using a primitive form of underwater radio communication with a submarine to help avoid the AMCs *Ebro*, *Artois* and *Moldavia* of the 10th Cruiser Squadron, patrolling nearby. Once it was realised by the British that she was out (only on 7 December), four AMCs from 10th Cruiser Squadron plus the light cruiser *Weymouth* were ordered to search for her. French vessels joined in and soon up to twenty-four warships were hunting for *Moewe*, in vain.

In four months she accounted for another twenty-five ships totalling 123,265 tons. Amongst her prizes were the Canadian Pacific steamship freighter *Mount Temple* on 6 December, which was outbound from Halifax to Liverpool. *Mount Temple* was notable for containing both war materiel and museum cargo. She held 700 horses bound for the Canadian Expeditionary Force in France and many crates of dinosaur fossils collected from Alberta's Red Deer River area by Charles H Sternberg (which were in transit to the British Museum of Natural History). Horses also featured in the capture on 12 December of SS *Georgic*, with 1,200 horses destined for the Western Front. Both ships and horses were sunk. A witness to the *Mount Temple* sinking noted that he saw 'the horses howling and struggling for life in the icy water'; hundreds of those from *Georgic* tried to swim to *Moewe* but 'German sailors standing with loaded revolvers killed them as they reached the ship'.

On 11 December Dohna-Schlodien took SS *Yarrowdale*. He saw potential in this vessel for conversion to a raider similar to *Moewe* and sent her as a prize to Swinemünde where she arrived on 31 December. She will be met again later in this book. A day after the capture of *Yarrowdale* he took *St Theodore*, which was converted there and then to an auxiliary cruiser and renamed *Geier* ('vulture'). She operated in the role for six weeks, accounting for further two ships sunk, before being scuttled by *Moewe* prior to her return home.

Twenty-four British cruisers and an unspecified number of

French vessels were now searching for her, ships which were badly needed in other areas of fleet operations as they fruitlessly scoured the North and South Atlantic. One single armed merchantman defied the power of the combined navies because of the fundamental difficulty of locating ships in the wide expanse of the ocean.

But the raider's luck could not hold forever. Eventually she must run up against a ship prepared to fight. On 10 March *Moewe* intercepted *Otaki*, a 9,575grt refrigerated cargo liner, owned by the New Zealand Shipping Company, sailing in ballast from London to New York and under the command of 38-year-old Captain Archibald Bisset Smith. Smith, an Aberdeenshire Scot now resident in New Zealand, had a stern-mounted 4.7in naval gun and he was unafraid to use it. When hailed to stop he refused and opened fire, causing significant damage to *Moewe* and starting a serious fire. Five German crewmen were killed and another ten men were wounded. With his own ship on fire and having suffered damage and casualties, Smith broke off the action and attempted to get his crew to the boats while the vessel sank under him. Six crew were lost, including Bisset Smith who, in the best seafaring tradition, went down with his ship.

Amongst the survivors was Smith's sixteen-year-old stepson, Alfred, who was on board with him and had tried to remain on the sinking vessel with his father, but Smith had forced him into a lifeboat.

For his courage (and perhaps *pour encourager les autres*) Captain Smith was awarded the Victoria Cross. As he was a civilian, and therefore not strictly entitled to receive the VC, Smith was posthumously gazetted a lieutenant in the Royal Naval Reserve. The citation noted that:

> During this action, the *Otaki* scored several hits on the *Moewe* causing considerable damage, and starting a fire, which lasted for three days. She sustained several casualties and received much damage herself, and was heavily on fire, Lieutenant Smith, therefore, gave orders for the boats to be lowered to allow the crew to be rescued. He remained on the ship himself and went down with her when she sank with the British colours still flying, after what was described in an enemy account as 'a duel as gallant as naval history can relate'.

Bisset Smith's wife was presented with his award in a ceremony at Buckingham Palace. The King told her that 'the country and himself were losers by the death of such a man as her husband'.

Bisset Smith's self-sacrifice saved others from the fate of sinking, for the damage he and his ship had inflicted forced the raider to return for Germany. *Otaki* had only managed to get eight shots away from her old gun (as opposed to thirty-two fired by the raider's armament), but they had been well placed. One had destroyed *Moewe's* port bow gun, another exploded in the saloon and started a fire, several hit and penetrated at the waterline, one cut a steam pipe in the stokehold and another lodged unexploded in the reserve bunkers. *Moewe* needed dockyard attention and Dohna-Shlodien recognised that his cruise was over.

In March 1917 *Moewe* again successfully ran the British blockade (see Chapter 18), having rendezvoused first with a U-boat which gave the latest dispositions of the Northern Patrol as far as known to the Imperial Navy. She arrived home safely on 22 March 1917 to another hero's welcome and was taken out of service as a propaganda tool too valuable to be risked again. During her service she had sunk a battleship and two cargo ships through her mining activities and taken by commerce raiding another forty vessels of a total 180,000grt (see Appendix 1), all under prize rules. No other German raider came close to her achievements and her success was celebrated in Germany through, inter alia, a film. In 1917 the imperial Bild und Filmamt in Berlin produced *Graf Dohna und seine Möwe*. It premiered at the Deutsches Opernhaus in Berlin on 2 May 1917.

The retirement of *Moewe* was nearly the end for the second phase of Germany's AMC commerce raiders. But there were some others of significance.

SMS *Meteor* just predated *Moewe*, and was an opportunistic conversion of a captured British vessel, *Vienna*, seized at Hamburg on the outbreak of war. Of typical English appearance she was armed with two 88cm guns (approx 3.5in), machine guns and 350 mines.

On 29 May 1915 *Meteor* set out on her first mission, to lay mines in the White Sea and attack Allied merchant ships transporting coal and other materiel to Russia. She sank three freighters and her mines accounted for three ships, all Russian. She returned unharmed in June 1915.

Her second mission, in August 1915, was to lay mines in the Moray Firth, but this was less successful. Attempting to pass through the Northern Blockade, she was challenged by the armed boarding vessel *Ramsey* (an Isle of Man steam packet built in 1895) on 9 August and ordered to stop for inspection. Whilst pretending to conform, *Meteor* was able to manoeuvre into a firing position while stopped, and suddenly opened devastating fire, quickly overwhelming *Ramsey*, which sank with the loss of fifty-three men. This was, however, a pyrrhic victory, for *Ramsey* had radioed a report of her attacker and several British cruisers were en route to assist. A German airship in the vicinity notified the captain of *Meteor* of his predicament and he scuttled the ship to avoid her capture. Before so doing he placed the survivors from his victim in a Swedish trawler, having first given them some money for essentials. In her brief career, *Meteor* had accounted for eight ships totalling 15,000 tons.

The loss of *Ramsey* was the first loss to a surface action for the Northern Patrol. Orders were quickly issued to the effect that more caution should be used:

> care is required when closing for boarding or examination and the gun and torpedo armament should be instantly ready. Bearings from which torpedoes can be fired [by the enemy] should be avoided: a good position from which to approach is on the quarter as rudder and screws can be watched.

Inspired by the success of *Moewe*, the German Navy converted a second, very similar ship, *Greif*, and fitted her with the same armament as carried by her predecessor. Originally named *Guben*, she was a 4,962grt steel-hulled steamship owned by the German-Australian Line (DADG) out of Hamburg. She sailed from Cuxhaven on 27 February 1916 under the command of Fregattenkapitän Rudolf Tietze.

However, hers was not to be a productive cruise, for the Royal Navy had learned of *Greif*'s sailing through radio intercepts and decoding. The 10th Cruiser Squadron was waiting for her in the North Sea.

Greif was disguised as the Norwegian *Rena* bound for Tønsberg, Norway, when she was intercepted by the 15,620-ton armed merchant cruiser *Alcantara* on the morning of 29 February. Unaccountably, perhaps bored by the quotidian task of boardings and search, *Alcantara* closed to 2,000yds and slowed to lower a boarding cutter (the more normal practice would have been to have stood off a greater distance) when *Greif* hoisted the German ensign, increased speed, and opened a withering and heavy fire. The first shell hit *Alcantara*'s bridge, disabling the telemotor steering gear, engine room telegraphs and all the telephones, as well as killing and wounding some key men. The boarding crew and their boat were literally blown to pieces. Hearing the gunfire, another AMC, *Andes*, headed towards the engagement and opened an effective fire from a range of over three miles.

The wounded *Alcantara* returned fire with her six 6in guns. The range was so close, never more than 3,000yds, and both ships wrought devastation on the other with their heavy weapons. *Greif* managed to launch a torpedo which hit *Alcantara* midship on the port side, and one of *Alcantara*'s shells exploded the ready-to-use ammunition for *Greif*'s after gun. The German ship was fighting a two-front battle, but she had inflicted mortal damage to *Alcantara*. Both ships lost way and *Greif*'s crew abandoned ship forty minutes after opening fire, but not before *Alcantara* had sunk with the loss of seventy-two men. *Andes* arrived to pick up survivors and as a final act, the light cruiser *Comus* and destroyer *Munster* (from the 4th Light Cruiser Squadron of the Grand Fleet, sent from Scapa to assist in the search) arrived in answer to radio broadcasts. They despatched the burning, disabled and stationary *Greif;* 187 Germans were killed, including her captain, who was beheaded by shrapnel while climbing down a rope into a lifeboat. Captain Thomas Wardle of *Alcantara* reported to the Grand Fleet that: 'I have the honour to report that the officers and men of HM Ship fought with great gallantry, and that no one left their stations until ordered to, and I personally witnessed cases of men assisting wounded at great risk'.

Both Commander Young of *Andes* and Captain Wardle of *Alcantara* were awarded the DSO for the action, in Wardle's case, despite the fact that he was court-martialled for losing his ship, criticised by his admiral for manoeuvring his vessel too close to the suspect, and the problem that the two captains' reports of the action 'differed in almost every respect'. Wardle was cleared by the court of any wrongdoing but Admiral de Chair (commanding 10th Cruiser Squadron) noted in a letter to Jellicoe that:

> the finding of the Court is satisfactory as regards the action of both *Alcantara* and *Andes*, but I am of opinion from the evidence given that *Andes* did not do all that was possible as to warning *Alcantara* that she was standing into danger, nor did the *Alcantara* take sufficient precautions in view of the warning as to the proximity of the raider; nevertheless both Captains, when they did grasp the situation, made the best of it and did very well.

In November 1916 another raider, *Wolf*, commenced a voyage of fifteen months, to South Africa, the Indian Ocean and Australia, in which she would sink fourteen ships and lay mines that destroyed fifteen more. *Wolf* was also able to extend her range with coal and supplies from her prizes, prolonging her voyage to a record-breaking fifteen months. She too outfitted a prize (commissioned as *Iltis*) to assist as an auxiliary, in this case as a minelayer. She returned home to a rapturous welcome having sunk 120,000 tons of shipping and, at one time or another, tied up British, Japanese and French ships to the sum of twenty-one cruisers, fourteen destroyers, nine sloops, the old battleship *Exmouth* and the seaplane carrier *Raven* in the search for her.

And in December 1916 the most unusual raider, *Seeadler* (Sea Eagle), set out, breaking through the Northern Patrol disguised as a Norwegian wood carrier, despite being stopped north of the Faroes on Christmas Day. It was perhaps in the spirit of giving that the boarding officer of HMS *Patia* failed to note the hidden weapons and German-speaking crew. She was a fully rigged sailing ship, a three-masted windjammer (though equipped with auxiliary motors), Scottish-built, taken as a prize when under an American flag and armed with two 10.5cm guns (approximately equivalent to a British 4in naval gun). *Seeadler* sailed to the South Pacific and sank sixteen ships for a total of 18,000 tons before being wrecked on a reef after eight months of operation. Her captain, Felix Graf von Luckner, another German aristocrat, was also unusual. He had begun by going round the world in a sailing vessel as a forecastle hand under the name of Phylax Luedicke; this included British-owned vessels which, in common with others of his kind, gave him an insight into the routes and methods of British ships. He had then passed the examination for an officer in the merchant marine, and finally through the influence of his family had entered the Imperial Navy. After serving on *Kronprinz* at the battle of Jutland, he was transferred to *Moewe* under Dohna-Schlodien, where he learned his trade from the master. His very unusual training had evidently been carefully noted by the German Admiralty. When they formed their plans for sending out raiders at the end of 1916, Luckner was one of the men they sent for.

Von Luckner's exploits earned him the epithet *Der Seeteufel* (the sea-devil) and his crew that of *Die Piraten des Kaisers* (the Emperor's pirates). Again he operated entirely under prize rules.

As for *Iltis*, captured and outfitted by *Wolf*, she had an ephemeral existence. She had begun life as the German freighter *Gutenfels* and was taken over by British forces in Alexandria at the outbreak of the war. Renamed *Turritella*, she was used as a merchant vessel until recaptured by *Wolf* in February 1917. Converted to a minelayer and with one 5.2cm gun, she was set loose on 27 February 1917, now renamed *Iltis* (Polecat), and was sent to Aden to lay a minefield. In the course of this mission she was sighted by the Royal Navy sloop *Odin* on the East Indian Station, an obsolete vessel, one of the last of the muddle of sloops and gunboats which characterised the Victorian navy, and armed with six 4in guns. After a long overnight stern chase from 2150 to 0545 on 5 March, *Iltis* lowered her boats and two loud explosions were heard. She had scuttled to avoid the ship being taken by the British once again and put to commercial use, having achieved no success in her five days of active life.

The raiders 'had seriously delayed shipping in various parts of the world, impeded the movement of troopships and attracted to themselves large numbers of Allied ships'. Indeed, the official historian wrote that the breakout of these AMCs at the end of 1916 was 'probably designed as a preliminary' to unrestricted submarine warfare, declared on 1 February 1917, and was intended to 'divert sizeable British cruiser forces from Atlantic and Home waters'.

PART TWO
Blockade

In August 1914 Britain had first to establish an effective blockade. Once that was in place, she had to overcome three key problems: an inadequacy of suitable vessels and manpower; a defensible legal basis for blockade; and American and other neutral opposition.

8

The Northern Patrol, 1914

Rear Admiral Dudley Rawson Stratford de Chair was born in Lennoxville, Canada, in 1864 to a family with a military background. Of Huguenot descent, his family could trace their ancestry back to a Jean de Chaire who was created a marquis on the field of battle by Henri IV of France. He joined the Royal Navy as a cadet aboard *Britannia* at Dartmouth in January 1878, where his term-mates for two years included Prince George, later King George V, and Prince Albert Victor, known as Eddie, George's elder brother.

De Chair served at the bombardment of Alexandria in 1882, where he was taken prisoner after volunteering to carry despatches to a desert fort. Brought before the rebel leader Arabi Pasha, he managed an adventurous escape. It transpired that Queen Victoria had requested prayers for his safety. On his return he showed his early promise by becoming a 'three-oner', three first-class passes in his lieutenant's exams (a rare and not entirely socially acceptable achievement, as intelligence was not necessarily the hallmark of a successful naval career). In fact, he eventually received five first-class certificates, which enabled him to reach lieutenancy without the intervening rank of sub lieutenant.

His career now followed an effortless upward course that included being personally recruited by Jellicoe, when Third Sea Lord and Controller of the Navy, to be his assistant controller and a spell as naval attaché to the United States from 1902–1905. During these years he again came in contact with royalty both in Britain and from abroad, as well as acquiring wealthy families such as the Vanderbilts as friends. De Chair, urbane and cultured, moved in high social circles and to nobody's surprise he became Naval ADC to his quondam classmate, King George V, in 1911 (succeeding Ernest Troubridge, another who had befriended the young and hapless prince at an early age).

In July 1912 de Chair was promoted a rear admiral and in January the following year he was invited by First Lord Winston Churchill to become his naval secretary. Although he accepted, he had mixed feelings about the post, seeing himself as a seaman first and foremost, and Churchill as a suspiciously self-seeking politician. The appointment was a challenging one, which he stuck at for eighteen months. Like so many sailors, he found Churchill's desire to take an executive role in day-to-day decisions somewhat trying and they had several stand-up rows. Churchill had promised de Chair the 2nd Cruiser Squadron at the end of his assignment, but in June 1914 he was appointed to the less than prestigious post of Admiral of the Training Service. This brought with it command of eight ageing *Edgar*-class cruisers. He was generally thought a lovely man, but was neither 'an inspiring leader or a strong character'.

Alexander Scrimgeour, who served as a midshipman on the cruisers *Crescent* and *Alsatian* with de Chair, described the admiral in 1914 as 'extremely nice, quiet, a perfect gentleman, but is, in my opinion rather oppressed and nervy … and relies very largely on Captain Trewby [flag captain] for his initiative'; later Scrimgeour wrote that 'he almost gives the impression of weakness'. By the crews, de Chair was nicknamed 'Old Make-a-Signal', owing to the large number of unnecessary signals he was thought to make.

As the outbreak of war became inevitable, the navy looked to fulfil its new strategy of distant blockade. The southern exits and entrances to the North Sea were closed off, however – as it transpired – porously, by the Harwich Force and the Dover Patrol, both mainly comprised of destroyers and light cruisers, and by minefields. The northern gateway, around Orkney, Shetland, Norway and Iceland, was intended, under a 1913 plan, to be sealed by the 10th and 11th Cruiser Squadrons. But the 11th, now designated Cruiser Force E, was sent instead first to Queenstown and then to the Persian Gulf, and de Chair's units, renamed as the 10th Cruiser Squadron, was all there was.

The Admiralty had issued orders for the fleet to prepare for war on 29 July, and on 1 August de Chair, who had been moving into his new house, left his wife amongst the packing cases and departed for Portsmouth. It would be more than two years before he saw the house again. The same day he raised his flag in *Crescent* and prepared to sail northwards. The indictment of Germany's trade, and the protection of Britain's, in the north now rested with de Chair and his ancient ships.

At 0400 on 3 August he was ordered to take his ships to Scapa Flow and he telegraphed Devonport, Chatham and Queenstown to collect up his scattered flock and set sail. Whilst still en route, the 10th Cruiser Squadron made their first capture, a large German steamship which tried to outrun them until a shot across the bows stopped her. She was *Wilhelm Behrens* with a cargo of timber and was sent to the Clyde under a prize crew. On 6 August *Endymion* and *Theseus* arrived, having been delayed in rounding up *Kronprinzessin Cecilie*, another German liner which was sent to Falmouth loaded with gold and specie. And on 7 August they had their first 'kill' when *Edgar* sank two German trawlers that refused to stop and tried to run.

The so-called Northern Patrol involved an area of sea covering the gap between the Orkney Isles and Norway, Shetland to Faroes, and Faroes to Iceland. Sea conditions in this region were always difficult and often dangerous. In summer there was frequent mist and sudden winds; in autumn, winter and spring there were fierce gales, raging seas, long, dark nights (in Orkney and Shetland it is dark early for nearly half the year), and heavy grey skies. Winds were frequently force 9 or 10 and the waves higher than the masts of the ships. Then there were what the local fishermen called 'the lumps': enormous waves, really two rolled into one, a big wave that captures the ones in front. In a force 10 wind with gusts up above 60 knots, visibility is hindered by the high waves and the spray from their crests; the monster 'lumps' are impossible to see coming until they strike, and when they do they can badly damage or occasionally sink even the most robust of vessels.

As an example, consider the ship's log of *Dryad*, an old (1893) torpedo gunboat, converted to minesweeper and attached to 10th Cruiser Squadron as a despatch boat. Her log entries demonstrate just how strong the winds could get, even when in so-called sheltered waters. Anchored in Loch Eriboll (a sea loch at the very top of the Scottish coastline and nicknamed Loch 'Orrible by the sailors for its weather), on 5 December 1914 she recorded winds of force 8–9 at 0400, 10–11 at 0800 and 8–9 again at 1600. And when off Long Hope in the Orkneys on 26 December she again experienced force 10–11 winds at noon. Force 11 is defined by the Beaufort Scale as 'Exceptionally high waves. Very large patches of foam, driven before the wind, cover much of the sea surface. Very large amounts of airborne spray severely reduce visibility. Widespread vegetation and structural damage likely.' Foul weather, indeed, to be looking for contraband runners. Truly, this was an inhospitable place to patrol.

By 7 August the squadron was at full strength, on its patrol line and designated Cruiser Force B. De Chair later described his mission as 'to intercept German vessels of war and German merchant vessels, and sink or capture them; also to stop all neutral vessels proceeding to German ports, and to deny the anchorage of any harbour in the Shetlands or Orkneys to the enemy'. Those ships patrolling in the vicinity of the Shetlands had frequently to pass the most northerly tip of the islands, the delightfully named Muckle Flugga. In honour of this lonely and forbidding piece of Britain they named themselves the Muckle Flugga Hussars.

To carry out his mission, de Chair had with him a force of antiques. Ten years old when Queen Victoria died, the *Edgar*s were obsolete, Victorian in design and philosophy. They were first-class protected cruisers, armed with two 9.2in guns and ten 6in quick-firers (*Crescent* and *Royal Arthur* were built to a slightly modified design with a raised forecastle and a pair of 6in guns replacing the forward 9.2in gun). Their armament reflected a different style of warfare, when captains were expected to close their enemy and pour in a barrage of shells from quick-firing weapons, and they had been intended to patrol the long sea-lanes of British imperial trade, keeping them free of molestation, showing the flag and sorting out the occasional restless natives. They had not been designed to keep constant station in dreadful sea conditions, intercepting ships that did not want to be caught. They were simply not up to the task. Neither were many of his crews of the first rank of the navy. Many were old pensioners, 'who had not expected that they would ever go to sea again, and now felt they might never see home again'.

Nonetheless, de Chair did his best. He eventually established a base, Swarbacks Minn,* in the Shetland Islands, and quartered his officers in billets there, including at the Hillswick Hotel (now the St Magnus Bay Hotel), which became an informal on-shore mess and officers club. And he set up his first patrols of four ships each, one to the Norway–Orkney gap and one to the Iceland–Faroe waters. The disadvantages of his ships soon became apparent. They were slow, took too long to reach their limited top speed and needed constant coaling, which meant that for each four-ship patrol, only three were on station at any time, the other being away refuelling.

Summer turned into autumn, and as the weather conditions changed from bad to atrocious, the ships began to fall apart. Reports emerged of weather being too bad for boarding to take place. Continuous running of the squadron brought on a bout of engineering problems. First to suffer was *Gibraltar*, with boiler problems; she was sent to the Tyne for docking. Soon *Royal Arthur* and *Crescent* needed defects repaired when next in for coaling.

And then the squadron suffered a tragedy. In early October 1914 de Chair was ordered further south as part of a plan to stop German warships, particularly submarines, from breaking out of the North Sea and attacking a troop convoy sailing from Quebec, comprising thirty-three Atlantic liners and bringing the Canadian Expeditionary Force (1st Canadian Division) to the UK (and which arrived safely in Plymouth Sound on 14 October).

On 15 October the 10th Cruiser Squadron was still on patrol off Aberdeen, deployed in line abreast at intervals of about ten miles. *Hawke* stopped at 0930 to pick up mail from sister-ship *Endymion*. After recovering her boat with the mail, *Hawke* proceeded at 13 knots without zigzagging to regain her station and was out of sight of the rest of the squadron when at 1030 a torpedo from the German submarine *U-9* struck her, and she quickly capsized and sank. The remainder of the squadron only realised there was a problem when,

---

* Swarbacks Minn is a roadstead between Vementry and Muckle Roe. Swarbacks Minn is located on the west coast of Shetland in the southeast corner of St Magnus Bay. The area incorporates Busta Voe, Aiths Voe, Olnafirth, Gonfirth, Northra Voe and Cole Deep. Some of the deepest inshore coastal waters in Shetland occur in the area – Swarbacks Minn itself is over a hundred metres deep in places.

after a further, unsuccessful, attack by *U-9* on *Theseus*, they were ordered to retreat at high speed to the northwest and no response to the order was received from *Hawke*. The destroyer *Swift* was dispatched from Scapa Flow to search for the missing ship and found a raft carrying one officer and twenty-one men, while a boat with a further forty-nine survivors was rescued by a Norwegian steamer; 524 officers and men died, including the ship's captain, H P E T Williams, with only seventy survivors.

The death of Captain Hugh Williams was particularly unfortunate as he was a rising star in the navy, a brave man who had gained a Royal Humane Society award for diving from the deck of his ship in 1895 to rescue a drowning stoker from the dark and squally waters of Milford Haven; and an intelligent man too, who gained four first-class passes in his lieutenant's exams. He had been noted for accelerated promotion and had held the rank of captain for less than a year.

Moreover, the loss of *Hawke* was controversial. Two hours before sailing, Captain Williams had gone on board *Crescent* to ask de Chair for an extra two days in harbour to repair his engines. Apparently, this was refused as the vessel was still capable of cruising at 10 knots; but at that speed she was a sitting duck for submarines when returning through the Moray Firth. Williams's last reported words as he left *Crescent* were, 'it is pure murder sending the ship with over 500 officers and men on board to sea in this state'. And so it proved.

The navy was a tight-knit community and when losses were incurred, officers and men thought of friends who might have been killed or rescued. Lieutenant Shuter in *Endymion* heard of the loss of *Hawke* on 16 October; his first thought was of his friend James 'Bunjy' H D Watson, who had played rugby for Blackheath and England and who was in her as a temporary surgeon. He was lost with the ship, aged just twenty-four years old and with three England caps to his credit. When *Bulwark* blew up with the loss of nearly all hands in November 1914, Shuter lost D H V Wilson, 'one of my best pals'. 'I knew heaps of officers in her', he confided to his diary.

On Trafalgar Day *Crescent* became involved in a surprise shooting match. A large oil tanker had been sighted NNW of Foula and a course was set to investigate it. She was wearing no colours and as the British ships closed, several shells suddenly whistled over her. The tanker was firing 4.1in guns at *Crescent*! General Quarters echoed round the ship and fire was opened at 7,000yds; but not before the mysterious stranger had shot away the portside water main and the foretop. The first British shots hit home, however, and a fire broke out on the tanker's deck; she speedily hoisted a white flag. It was too rough to send over a boarding party so de Chair signalled in International Code that the tanker should consider herself a prize and she was convoyed to Lerwick. There she was discovered to be a Norwegian steamer bought two months previously by the German navy to act as a long-distance submarine depot ship: a worthwhile capture, indeed.

The engineering problems continued. On 29 October *Grafton* reported the main condenser leaking and its funnels as showing signs of weakness. Next to suffer was *Theseus* the same day. She had broken down in general chase with her sister-ship *Endymion*. On 31 October *Theseus* again reported defects. These included a rupture to the reserve feed water tanks, bilge water leaking into feed tanks and the water density of boilers rapidly increasing. She was ordered back to Swarbacks Minn for self-repair. *Endymion* reported her arrival at Scapa Flow and also that she could not leave as there were serious defects in the engines and fore bridge. *Crescent* reported a leaky condenser. Then on 11 November *Edgar* reported serious engine defects and was ordered back to base for repairs if and when the weather improved.

And still the patrol work continued; and additionally Jellicoe, in command of the Grand Fleet at Scapa Flow, made frequent requests for sweeps outside of de Chair's designated patrol areas.

The weather continued to be vile. On 2 November Scrimgeour confided to his diary that:

the weather up here is so uniformly bad that in future I shall only remark in my diary when it is good, which I expect will be very seldom, as the only variation to the prevailing southwest gales with rain and big seas is a biting cold northerly wind coming straight down from the Arctic Circle and Spitzbergen.

And on 11 November de Chair's flagship, *Crescent*, shipped a monster wave – a lump – over the forecastle which completely carried away the admiral's sea cabin (fortunately he was not in it), swept a whaler from its davits, and swamped an engine room ventilator, putting out fires in several boilers. In the same storm *Edgar* also reported an able seaman and a cutter swept overboard. Waves reached forty or fifty feet high, and winds maintained force 10–11 for eight hours. De Chair afterwards admitted that 'we really did not think the old ship could weather it'.

On board *Endymion*, Shuter noted 'an awful middle watch, howling and pelting with rain', and the following day 'kept the forenoon watch. Stinking weather ... awfully bad, very big wind and sea'.

Crescent, *Royal Arthur* and *Grafton* were ordered to the Clyde for investigation and repairs; these were actually put in hand, with the object of getting the vessels seaworthy by early December. The patrol was now minimal and it was clear that, as currently constituted, the 10th Cruiser Squadron could not carry out its task. Discussions held with the director of dockyards pointed out the hopelessness of the position and the law of diminishing returns which applied to the repairs planned. On 20 November the Admiralty ordered all remaining seven *Edgar*s to return to their home ports to be paid off. Their ordeal was over.

The old cruisers had never really been up to the mission given. But nonetheless, in less than five months they had boarded over three hundred ships and intercepted many others in rough seas. Without them, how was the blockade to be carried on?

9

Enter the Merchantmen, 1914–1915

The navy turned to a class of ship that had been specifically designed with the objectives of long endurance, high speed and good sea-keeping qualities – the passenger liner and fast cargo vessel, now designated as Armed Merchant Cruisers (AMCs). The use of AMCs had been considered by the Admiralty before the war and contingent plans made in a War Office staff paper of April 1914, which highlighted some of the ships they would like to take over as soon as war was declared. Thus *Alsatian*, *Mantua* and *Teutonic** were all commissioned in August 1914 and sent to assist the 10th Cruiser Squadron, being on station by 18 August. *Alsatian* was quickly in the thick of the action. On one day, 25 August, she boarded five vessels between 0600 and 1855, three Norwegian, one Swedish and one British. Overall, the experience gained from these merchant ships gave comfort to the idea that, as a class of vessel, they could be very useful for patrol purposes.

Initially, the AMCs operated under a system whereby a Royal Navy officer became the ship's commanding officer and the vessel's original captain stayed on as second in command with the rank of commander RNR, judged necessary because of the difficulties of handling ships of such a size. Such a system was likely to cause problems and on 8 September 1914 the ex-RMS *Oceanic*, a huge liner of 17,247 tons under the joint command of RN Captain W F Slayter and her original master, Henry Smith, was patrolling in the

---

*Teutonic was the first British commercial vessel to have been specially designed to act as an AMC in wartime. Billed as an armed merchantman, she had been present at the 1889 Spithead review in honour of the German Kaiser and had been inspected by him.

region of the Shetlands when she ran aground off Foula Island and foundered.

Captain Slayter had retired after taking the night watch, unaware that the navigator had made an inaccurate fix of their position the previous day and that they were already too close to the Isle of Foula and on the wrong side of it, and left orders to steer for the island. Commander Smith took over the morning watch and felt that the vessel would be better in open sea. Having previously disagreed with his naval superior about dodging around the island, he instructed the navigator to plot a course out to sea. Slayter reappeared on the bridge and countermanded Smith's order, which turned out to be a poor decision, for it resulted in the ship running directly onto the Shaalds. She was wrecked in a flat calm and clear weather. *Oceanic* was thus the first Allied passenger ship to be lost in the war. She had been in commission as an AMC for exactly a month.

At the subsequent court martial the navigator was blamed and both captains exonerated, but the court martial made very clear that the position of the original ship's master was that of second in command and that he acted solely in an advisory capacity.

With the demise of the *Edgars*, de Chair shifted his flag to *Alsatian* on 4 December. With him came Flag Captain Trewby, Fleet Paymaster Lawford, a secretary, and Flag Lieutenant Commander Robinson, his personal coxswain and a servant. *Alsatian* was an Allan Line transatlantic passenger liner, launched in 1912, of 18,481grt, 571ft and with a speed of 18 knots. She had only come into service in spring 1914 and, amongst other delights, was designed to carry 287 first-class passengers in style. *Alsatian* and the three other AMCs had been attached to the 10th Cruiser Squadron for four months. Now they were to *be* the 10th! De Chair was no doubt pleased to leave the battered and bruised old cruiser *Crescent* for the more salubrious accommodation of the first-class lounge, especially as initially his new charges were based out of Liverpool because of the lack of suitable coaling facilities on the Shetlands.

Alsatian was originally armed with eight 4.7in and two 6pdr guns and crewed by sixty-seven officers and 480 crew. The armament was upgraded to 6in guns in Liverpool in December.

However, the acceptance trials went badly and she did not leave to return to her station in the north until 23 December. In this month, de Chair's new AMC-based squadron was still under refit – eight at Liverpool, four in London, five at Avonmouth and one each in Hull, Tyne and Clyde. The Northern Patrol at this time existed only on paper!

With the exception of the captain, one or two officers, the gunner and the boatswain who were Royal Navy, the crews of these AMCs were reservists, volunteers or under special articles, usually men who had served the ship in civilian life. The *Liverpool Courier* recorded the process:

> Liverpool's contribution was not only in ships, but men, for as the crews of the vessels were paid off by the companies on the transfer of the vessel to the Admiralty, they proceeded to the naval depot which Admiral Stileman [Rear Admiral Harry Hampson Stileman, SNO Liverpool] had established and signed on under special naval articles, for service in their old ship, whilst the officers and engineers, being almost entirely R.N.R. men, were usually transferred to the active list and appointed to the ship as soon as she had been commissioned under a Royal Navy captain.

However, not everyone in Liverpool shared de Chair's sense of urgency to get the merchant ships converted and on duty. Trouble was experienced with the trade union, which ordered a strike because 'a man who was using his acetylene blow lamp on one of the gun mountings did not have the authorised number of men sitting down watching him work'. The admiral was incensed: 'I was full of fury that … these pro-enemy loafers who stayed on shore should batten on the seamen who were protecting their homes.' De Chair sent for the head of the union; in fact, he sent an armed guard to fetch him. When the hapless official arrived, de Chair told him that 'if the men working on board the ships of the 10th Cruiser Squadron were not at work within the hour he would be put in prison'. This had the desired effect.

Alsatian was joined by other AMCs (forty-one were to serve at various times on the Northern Patrol in total – see Appendix 2 –

twenty-seven of which were Liverpool-based ships in civilian times) similarly armed and crewed, and the 10th Cruiser Squadron was reconstituted as a force of armed merchant cruisers, with twenty-four generally under orders at any one time.

Originally intended to be armed with obsolete 4.7in guns of nineteenth-century vintage, the AMCs were finally fitted with (generally) eight 6in guns, as the smaller weapons had proven to be less than effective against the sort of ships they were likely to have to fight. The problem of fitting a suitably safe magazine for the guns' shells was solved by building large steel tanks in the fore and aft holds with appropriate arrangements for flooding and ventilating in case of fire. In some cases cofferdams were additionally built around these tanks as further protection. Ammunition supply to the weapons was problematic as there were no shell hoists and in the end it was stacked around the guns on deck: a highly dangerous situation when under fire! The risk entailed was illustrated by *Teutonic* when a 6in shell on deck in the ready-use rack came loose due to heavy seas and partially exploded against the bulwarks, damaging the ship.

Gunnery control was by voice-pipe with accuracy depending solely on the skills of the individual gunlayers. Gun crews were kept permanently closed up when on patrol and it was thus soon discovered necessary to build special shelters near their weapons for protection against the elements.

Given the considerable vulnerability of the AMCs when under fire, owing to their great size and lack of armour, much attention was paid to safety and 'abandon ship' drills and, in addition, buoyancy was enhanced by stowing large amounts of timber and empty metal drums below the waterline. On patrol, ship's boats were always kept swung out, fully watered and provisioned. It was perhaps not just irony that led to the sailors nicknaming them 'Admiralty Made Coffins'.

All the cargo space in the lower holds was filled with coal. *Alsatian*, for example, carried an additional 5,600 tons over and above that in her normal bunkers, which were themselves never allowed to drop below 500 tons to aid stability. Whilst on patrol, all boilers were kept lit and a cruising speed of between 10 and 13 knots maintained.

The bonus for the ordinary sailor of service on board an AMC, was that the accommodation was a considerable improvement on that found in regular naval vessels. Peacetime public rooms were converted into messes, lounges, smoking rooms and places of assembly. The ship's company lived and slept in the passenger cabins and the space previously allocated to the ship's peacetime crew was used for storage. As one ship's captain noted on taking over his vessel, 'I went to bed well satisfied with the comfort I am surrounded with.'

All the ships to be used as AMCs were chartered from the owners by the Admiralty, which also carried all the insurance risk, at the generous rate of around 20 shillings per gross ton per month. Thus *Alsatian* cost the exchequer some £222,000 per annum (circa £19 million in today's money), which represented a good return for the owners. On 4 July 1915 twenty-four such ships were serving in the 10th Cruiser Squadron at a monthly cost to the taxpayer of £222,354, before the cost of manning and provisioning: 7,330 officers and men, mostly RNR, were employed aboard them.

As an example of the workload of these chartered ships, in the six months from 25 December 1914 *Alsatian* had steamed 35,758 miles and had been under way 138 days: she had consumed 20,796 tons of coal and 13,322 tons of water. The squadron as a whole consumed 1,600 tons of coal a day.

The formidable logistics necessary to maintain such a supply chain meant that in the early days of 1915 the squadron had to be based at Liverpool, four days steaming from their patrol area, and which meant that half of the ships were away heading to or from coaling at any one time. This was clearly massively inefficient. It was also not particularly safe.

For example, after five weeks on patrol, *Alsatian* returned to Liverpool and leave in January 1915, but found herself unable resume her duties as German submarines were reported off Bardsey Isle on 29 January. By midday they were seen off the Bar and clearly were going to make life difficult or impossible for those ships of the 10th still in harbour to leave the shelter of the River Mersey.

On 30 January three merchantmen were sunk off the Bar and the following day three German submarines accounted for eleven merchant ships. All Royal Navy ships were instructed to remain in Liverpool, all sailing orders were postponed and the port of Liverpool was declared closed to merchant shipping. The squadron's vessels returning for coaling were diverted by radio to the Clyde and the big liners to Southampton; the patrol had, to all intents and purposes, ceased to exist thanks to the activities of only three U-boats. Loch Ewe also played host to some of the squadron, much to the disgust of the sailors on board who had been looking forward to a run ashore in the 'Pool'.

On 1 February a torpedo-boat flotilla arrived from Pembroke to attempt to clear the passage: de Chair ordered yachts, trawlers and an Isle of Man packet to be commandeered and fitted with 6pdr guns to reinforce the hunting party. But on 3 February the ships of the 10th Cruiser Squadron were still trapped and, to make matters worse, *Calyx* burst into flames and was still burning at midnight. *Alsatian* and the others finally got away the following day.

De Chair yearned and agitated to get back to his old base at Swarbacks Minn, but the Admiralty were opposed. Given the constant calls upon him to cover the west coast of Scotland too, de Chair won through and the desirability of a base in the north was finally accepted. De Chair went to Swarbacks Minn on 19 June for a conference with Rear Admiral Fawckner who had been appointed Senior Naval Officer, Swarbacks Minn, in May. Representatives of the works and store departments also attended and arrangements were made for coaling and watering. The old *Edgar*-class cruiser *Gibraltar* was sent to become a depot and repair ship. The hospital ship HMHS *Berbice*, built in 1909 as a 2,379grt Royal Mail steam packet serving the inter-island mail and cruising trade of the Caribbean, was despatched and based off Delting in Busta Voe to cater for the sick and wounded. And the twenty-four ships of the squadron left the fleshpots of Liverpool for the austerity of the Shetland Islands.

1 0

The Volunteers

The 10th Cruiser Squadron and its merchant cruisers were largely manned by volunteers, Royal Naval Reserve (RNR) and increasingly, as the war progressed, Royal Naval Volunteer Reserve (RNVR).

At the outbreak of war, the ships of the Royal Navy were divided into three fleets. The First Fleet was the core of the navy, efficient modern ships, fully crewed by Royal Navy officers and men, constantly ready for deployment. The Second Fleet was effectively a naval reserve, ships that the Admiralty no longer wanted in the line of battle, but for which there might be a need in time of war and which could be counted in the total numbers of the fleet. They were 'retired' to port where they were kept ticking over by a reduced crew of about 60 per cent of the required complement (called a nucleus crew); in time of war or for exercises with the main fleet, the crew could quickly be brought up to strength by drafting men from the nearby naval barracks, reservists, and boys in training. Primarily, the driver was to reduce the cost of keeping them in commission. The Third Fleet was a miscellaneous collection of the antique, the obsolescent and the obsolete. They were crewed by a much reduced care and maintenance party (C&M). When war was declared they were plucked off the dockyard wall and crewed mainly with reservists and boys.

Volunteers were thus critical to the effective staffing of the navy. The Royal Naval Reserve (RNR) and the Royal Fleet Reserve (RFR) were naval reserves forces drawn from professional officers and ratings of the mercantile marine and ex-naval ratings. Membership of the former was voluntary, but many major mail steamer companies encouraged their employees to join. After basic training, further periodic training with the fleet was undertaken. The latter was a force drawn from former naval ratings who, after completing their contractual service with the Royal Navy, were liable to recall in times of emergency. The liability lasted for a specified number of years after leaving active service in the navy. In both instances a royal proclamation was required to call up the personnel in times of emergency.

The empire, too, provided reservists. In Newfoundland, for example, an RNR service had been formed in 1903. Acceptance required that candidates be seamen or fishermen between the ages of eighteen and thirty. All men enrolled for five years and completed twenty-eight days' drill annually. By August 1914 the reserve had a strength of over five hundred men, of whom 75 per cent were classified as qualified seamen, having trained at sea, passed an elementary examination in gunnery and seamanship, and been recommended by the commanding officer. De Chair later wrote, '[the] Newfoundland fishermen turned out to be some of our best boatmen in boarding prizes in heavy seas'. Twenty-five men from the Newfoundland division of the RNR died when *Viknor* went down (*vide infra*). They are remembered on the Beaumont Hamel memorial in France (where the Newfoundland Regiment of their countrymen had been wiped out on the Somme).

And so it was, when on 2 August the proclamation for full naval mobilisation went out, the reserves responded. The navy's manpower strength in August 1914 stood at only 147,667 men. In Hull and Grimsby, at the East Anglian fishing ports, in the fishing communities of the southwest, thousands of reservists were called up by telegram, delivery boys or policemen knocking on their doors. In Brixham, nearly every family was affected by mobilisation and the town's annual regatta was abandoned. Men were commanded to report to the customs house on the quay and depart for the naval barracks at Devonport. The cottage hospital nurses turned out to cheer them off and the chairman of the urban district council presided over the singing of the national anthem at the railway station. In Looe, Cornwall, the men mustered on the quay and were marched to the railway station. In Falmouth the call-up was announced by the town crier. The navy girded its loins.

Mobilisation of the reserves added 31,107 Royal Fleet Reservists and 19,080 Royal Naval Reserve. Included in the RFR call-up were 8,327 retired officers and pensioners who stepped forward once more for duty.

There were also 4,500 Royal Navy Volunteer Reserves initially called up. The Royal Naval Volunteer Reserve was another naval reserve force of men drawn from civilian occupations ashore. They were enthusiastic volunteers and not professional seafarers, somewhat similar to the Territorial Army. The volunteers carried out training in the evenings, at weekends and two weeks' annual training aboard naval ships or at naval establishments. All officers were promoted from the lower deck. They could be yachtsmen, clerks, fishermen, inshoremen, accountants, bankers (one company in London was composed entirely of stockbrokers) – any walk of life or profession. They were looked down upon by the professional navy (who gave them the soubriquet 'wavy navy' after the design of the stripes of rank), but during the course of the war they progressively replaced RNR men in smaller ships, freeing the more experienced sailors for the larger vessels. Over 32,000 RNVR ratings served during the course of the war.

Men from the Scottish islands (Shetlands and Orkneys in particular) and trawlermen were especially prized for their skills in handling small craft, nowhere more so than in the 10th Cruiser Squadron for the difficult task of launching a small boat into dangerous seas to board a potential contraband runner. According to a post-war magazine, 'Many of the RNVR officers came from overseas, notably from New Zealand, to act as skippers and junior officers of the innumerable motor launches'; 23 per cent of the male population of New Zealand served in the war, 4.1 per cent died.

A large proportion of the RNVR was originally incorporated into the Royal Naval Division for service ashore in the attempted relief of Antwerp in 1914, but increasingly the RNVR men came to man the vessels of the various auxiliary patrols and the many trawlers and drifters which the navy had taken over for minesweeping and anti-submarine duties. Armed yachts and motor launches also relied largely on the wavy navy for their crews.

Finally, there was the Mercantile Marine Reserve (MMR). This encompassed Mercantile Fleet Auxiliaries (MFAs; merchantmen on government service), and was divided into two parts. There were those vessels which were non-commissioned, which meant that they were on time-charter to the government and their crews remained subject to the usual civilian legislation of the Board of Trade, the Merchant Shipping Acts. Secondly, there were the commissioned MFAs (the category to which the AMCs of the 10th Cruiser Squadron belonged). They were operated in a different manner, their owners having little to do with them, and were classed as naval auxiliaries, flying the white ensign. Instead of commercial articles, officers and men of these vessels signed T.124 forms (see Appendix 3 for an example), binding them to the Naval Discipline Act, as was seen in Chapter 9 for the civilian vessels transferring to AMC status at Liverpool.

From diaries and letters of the period, it would appear that there were tensions between the Royal Navy men and their reserve colleagues and that it took time for the RNR, RFR, MMR and RNVR sailors to gain acceptance and respect. For some professional navy men that respect did not ever dawn. As an example, here is Commander Brocklebank RN of *Changuinola*: 'I have been at sea in this ship for over two years now and feel myself sinking to the level of the RNR, good fellows, worthy and honest though they be, constant association with them does not tend to liven any brain or thoughts one may have.'

Midshipman Scrimgeour was also unimpressed with his new RNR midshipmen colleagues (in peacetime, apprentices in various liners): 'they are rather uncouth in their manners and hardly what the world calls gentlemen,' he noted.

And some captains clearly resented having to command ships with reserve officers under them. In 1915 de Chair was moved to write to all his captains, 'it has come to my ears that some of the captains of ships of the 10th CS are not treating their RNR officers very well'. Some RNR and RNVR officers were reported as saying that 'they had joined for the period of the war and were very glad they had done so but they would be d....d if they would be bullied by naval officers'.

Commander Grenfell, the number one of *Cedric*, believed the main culprit within the 10th Cruiser Squadron to be Booty of *Otway*. Booty, aged fifty-three at the time and an MVO, was the second most senior captain in the squadron in 1915 and had previously been the captain of the Portsmouth navigation school. He was a sailor of the old school. 'At any rate, it is most unfortunate,' Grenfell confided to his diary.

By way of digression, Francis Henry Grenfell serves as an example of the sometimes strange routes by which men came to be in the 10th Cruiser Squadron. Born in 1874, he entered *Britannia* in 1889 and was one of the last officers to undertake a foreign commission under sail. When work aloft was removed from the training agenda, the Admiralty introduced physical training into the curriculum and Grenfell was appointed lieutenant in the physical training school at Portsmouth. There he developed such a passion for the 'Swedish system', which formed the basis for instruction that he wrote a book about it (*The Swedish System of Education for Gymnastics*) in 1905 and in the same year retired from the navy to teach the subject in public schools, subsequently joining the Board of Education in 1909 to undertake the same mission for state schools.

On the outbreak of war he was recalled to the navy, aged forty with the rank of lieutenant commander on the retired list (commander in December 1914). He was appointed second in command to Commodore R E R Benson in *Cedric* (a 21,035grt ex-White Star Line transatlantic liner built in 1902) in October 1915.

Another problem was pay differences, which were an important source of regular navy dissatisfaction. In 1914 the average monthly rate of pay for a mercantile able seaman in Liverpool was £5 10s. In the Royal Navy an AB received £2 18s (which had only increased by 2d per day since 1852). What is more, an agreement was made to pay £1 a month above the port rates in the union's book for 1913 to retain or recruit mercantile marine ratings as a reward for added danger and their patriotism in volunteering. Additionally, those RNR members who were called up from the merchant service only received RN rates and thus suffered a pay cut. The RN sailors hence always considered the mercantile ratings as overpaid for apparently similar work. The situation was compounded by the fact that mercantile ratings who had signed on via the T.124 articles, and RNR ratings mobilised at the beginning of the war, soon found that sailors who had remained aboard ordinary trading vessels (and were thus thought to be to be less patriotic), quickly overtook the '£1 a month above port rates' by subsequent negotiated war bonuses, widening the gap still further (although their pay ceased if their ship was sunk).

These issues were never really addressed properly (not least because in the beginning everyone expected a short war) and caused an ongoing headache for de Chair and his staff. Admiral Stileman at Liverpool wrote to the Admiralty:

> Authority is requested to place all mercantile ratings at present serving in HM Ships visiting Liverpool on the port rates as at present or as may in future prevail. To complete the crew of HMS *Andes* the present rates will have to be paid, and I anticipate that should different scales of pay prevail in the same ship, wholesale desertions will ensue in all ships affected.

Before this plea, de Chair had written to the director of trade division, who in turn passed the query to the director of transports:

> The conditions under which some of the Armed Merchant Cruisers, more particularly *Alsatian*, have been taken up are not quite clear, and the arrangements laid down in 'Instructions regarding Armed Merchant Cruisers' do not appear to have been followed as far as engagement, crews, messing and complements etc., are concerned. If you can supply any information on these points, it would be of assistance to Captains who are at present not sure of their powers ...

It was a mess, and remained one throughout; that a war could be fought in this confusion must be seen as admirable.

The boiler room firemen, generally all RFR (ex-merchant marine), were a particular source of trouble. Commander Brocklebank of *Changuinola* noted in his diary in 1915, 'a fireman had written a note on their messdeck "this dammed rot must cease". So I had an interview with all the firemen after quarters and gave them all to understand my views on their duties'. And England of *Orvieto* recorded that he 'made an oration to the firemen which I hope will do them no harm'.

Lieutenant Alexander McGill RNVR of *Teutonic* recorded in his diary the trouble that could break out over the issue of Royal Navy rather than Merchant Navy 'terms and conditions'. In late 1916 he noted that whilst in dock at Liverpool:

the ships firemen [Mercantile Marine Reserve men] refused to work, citing they wanted merchant steamer food and not navy rations. The Admiral of the Port [Admiral Stileman] was called and he brought 50 armed guards with him. He called each man out and asked if he would do his duty or not. Eight refused and were marched off the ship to face a court martial.

The courts martial were held a fortnight later. Each took around half an hour, and a sentence of two years' imprisonment at Devonport was handed down to all the offenders. McGill noted that 'Admiral Tupper [who replaced de Chair in 1916] came on board a few days after and gave them [the firemen] a speech about not grumbling too much and doing their duty.'

Overall, however, de Chair was fulsome in his endorsement of the work of his reserve sailors.

Although there is an adequate sprinkling of Royal Navy men in command, by far the majority of blockade officers are drawn from the Royal Naval Reserve. These men, many of whom have had splendid careers in the British Mercantile Marine, are peculiarly fitted for blockade work; they are accustomed to manifests and ships' papers; they know how to make a quick, comprehensive and judicial inspection of cargoes.

Admiral Tupper commented, 'Man-o-war routine was entirely strange to these men, but, taking it all round, the discipline of the lower decks of the Tenth Cruiser Squadron was excellent.'

And Admiral Bacon, in charge of the Dover Patrol and channel blockade for much of the war noted:

Look at the way our fisher-folk crowded to our fleets to do the hard sea work to which their lives at sea had inured them, and for which the Navy had neither the vessels nor the men. As the crews of the old Cinque Port vessels and the volunteer fleet had crowded to the flag when invasion by Frenchmen or Spaniard threatened; so our fisher-folk and men of the Merchant Navy, Royal Naval Reserve and Royal Naval Volunteer Reserve rallied unarmed to do our auxiliary work in the Great War.

And so the 10th Cruiser Squadron fought its war with a complement of retired navy men, merchant seamen, coastguards (known as 'gobbies' in the navy), passenger liner crews, keen volunteers, fishermen, and men from the far-flung British Empire. Men who understood the navy and men who were bamboozled by it; men who knew the sea and its many moods, and men who knew only the creeks and rivers of England; men who knew that the sea could kill them, and men who didn't know how or why they died.

11

Captains Courageous

The mix between regular Royal Navy men and the reservists and merchant sailors who crewed the ship was a challenging one, which initially taxed the 10th Cruiser Squadron and called for considerable efforts from the ship's captains, all of whom were captains or commanders RN. It took time to get the ships into martial shape, and the long cruises in difficult seas, the problems of putting aboard the boarding parties, and the political ramifications of the treatment of neutrals all demanded skill and concentration which was possibly not called for in the regular Royal Navy service. Additionally, unlike a 'traditional' posting, a captain could not rely on having other RN men around and serving under him, whose reactions, understanding and skill-set he could broadly predict.

As an example, Captain Valentine Egerton Bagot Phillimore (who had won the DSO in the Boxer rebellion) had commissioned *Alsatian* as a warship in 1914. For his commander, his second in command who was expected to present the ship to him as a fighting unit, he had the ship's last master, Captain E Outram RNR, and his chief engineer was Robert Wilson, her peacetime engineering officer. For these latter officers, brought up in the merchant service where saving the owners' money on fuel and repairs was a religion, it must have come as a shock to see their beautiful charges so roughly treated (but they got used to it and all three were eventually awarded the DSO for their services, personally presented by the King). When de Chair made *Alsatian* his flagship he brought with him his flag captain, Captain George Trewby, who had commanded *Crescent*, and Phillimore was moved to *Motagua*. Trewby's commander on

Crescent had been John Kiddle, a regular officer plucked from retirement for the war and he came over to *Alsatian* too, the flagship needing rather more of a sprinkling of Royal Navy men.

But the general rule was that the ships' crews were almost entirely volunteers and reservists. *Kildonan Castle* in August 1916 serves as an exemplar. Her captain was a regular officer. But under him the first lieutenant and gunnery lieutenant were lieutenant commanders RNR, the navigator was a lieutenant RNR, as were the five other lieutenants and sub lieutenants on board. The chief gunner was a regular warrant officer, the wireless operators were RNR, the surgeon was a regular, his assistant RNVR, as was the paymaster, and there were seven RNR midshipmen on board too. Of the whole officer suite there were only three regulars, including the captain.

On *Changuinola*, of nineteen officers only four were regular navy; amongst the petty officers and men there were twenty-two RN, forty-two RFR, thirty-five RNR and fifteen RNVR. Of twenty-five Marines, sixteen were reservists and three were pensioners – and she carried an amazing sixty-three civilians, including cooks and stewards.

Bringing this mix of experiences together and creating a fighting unit was a tough job. Commander George Plunkett England commissioned *Orvieto*, taking her over at the Royal Albert Dock, London, in July 1916. He noted in his diary that he 'would have preferred a flotilla leader but beggars can't be choosers', a preference probably shared by all his colleagues. Five days later he had to replace his (RNR) navigator, and expressed frustration at the difficulties that he was having with ciphers and codes owing to the 'inexperience of signalmen and WT ratings'. In his ship's company of 300 men he reckoned to have only thirty real seamen and 'one ancient looking signalman is by profession a musician in a Brighton orchestra'.

Meanwhile, on *Kildonan Castle*, fire practice off Shoeburyness elicited a letter of complaint to the Admiralty from a farmer whose fields had been ploughed up by errant 6in practice shells from the ship. And when *India* first tested her guns, it 'broke windows all over the deck and wrecked the midshipmen's cabins'.

Some captains worked hard to keep their crews at a high level of motivation amongst the difficulties of the weather and the duties. Commander H C R Brocklebank, who had commissioned the ex-banana vessel *Changuinola* (named for a city in Panama) at

Avonmouth on Christmas Eve 1914, was particularly noted for his efforts in this regard. He placed considerable emphasis on the efficiency of his boarding boats' crews – in many respects his 'weapons' in the role – and his vessel was considered the 'crack ship' in this regard. He also put much effort into keeping the men occupied and happy. The ship had a rudimentary gymnasium and Brocklebank organised all-ship sports competitions on deck when weather permitted. Prizes were presented, small cash awards for the ratings and replica Iron Crosses for the officers, which caused great amusement below decks. One sailor by name of Karr entered many competitions but won none. He was presented with a brass cross with 'nil desperandum' inscribed on it. One seaman, in his memoirs, noted that 'it was pleasant to have such a good feeling between the officers and men'.

This was not the case on other ships of the squadron. *Changuinola*'s officers, when sent for duty aboard other vessels, reported that some ships had no recreation at all; their attitude seemed to be 'we are at war and must therefore be miserable'.

In his efforts, Brocklebank was aided by having Lieutenant John Shuter as his first lieutenant and second in command. Shuter's father was a noted Surrey and England cricketer, who went on to be a Test selector before the war, and young John had inherited his father's passion for sports. His diary records that he boxed with his fellow officers nearly every day, walked miles whenever ashore, and taught Swedish gymnastics on board ship. It was he who had converted the ship's smoking room into a makeshift gym.

Brocklebank's methods did not always keep men out of trouble; in January 1917 he had to formally reprimand a junior officer, Assistant Paymaster Reginald Houghton, for being drunk on *Orvieto*.

Shuter and Brocklebank were responsible for commissioning the ship and fortunately they got on well. So well, indeed, that Shuter's sister Phyl, who lived in Southsea, went to live with Mrs Brocklebank in Weybridge for the duration.

Commissioning was a difficult experience. Shuter wrote on 29 December 1914: 'working hard all day trying to get things shipshape. Took some marines at 3.30 ... the lights in my cabin fused ... A thoroughly trying day and I was glad when it was over'. The following day produced the laconic diary entry, 'another trying day'. For 31 December he recorded, 'another awful day for me'.

The ship celebrated the arrival of the New Year in the traditional naval fashion, rattling tin cans down the ladders and at midnight striking sixteen bells – eight bells for the old year and eight bells for the new – to welcome the first morning of 1915. This did not, however, improve Shuter's state of mind. On New Year's Day he recorded 'feeling rather moody'. And when they finally got to sea Shuter's lot did not improve: on 10 and 11 January the steering telemotor broke down, necessitating steering by use of the engines, and it broke down again two days later.

On patrol, the workload they got through was formidable. Commander Brocklebank noted in his diary that during 1915 his ship had boarded 159 ships, sent fifty of them to port for inspection and spent only ninety-four nights in harbour. That means that he boarded a ship once every 1.7 days at sea, including time spent getting to and from the patrol areas.

The job of the captains of these AMCs was not assisted by the Admiralty's almost total lack of knowledge concerning the characteristics and build qualities of passenger liners and merchant ships, as opposed to 'grey navy' vessels.

Shortly after commissioning his ship, Brocklebank of *Changuinola* cabled the Admiralty asking for 300 tons of ballast to be made available for him when he docked at Liverpool. In response, the Admiralty asked him for a full report as to why he needed it as they 'did not consider the stability of the ship necessitates any ballast'. Brocklebank fulminated that that meant he would have to wait months before he could get some. He went on, 'it is not the stability of the ship that is wrong but the trim. She is down by the stern and should be on an even keel and when very light of coal her handling in heavy weather may be awkward'.

He wrote home despairingly, 'the ship is somewhat unmanageable ... she is light forward and her bows act like a headsail'. Then the fitment of a new 6in gun forward in December 1916 caused the opposite problem: 'New gun and great weight of structure makes the ship dive heavily and take in big seas,' he confided to his diary.

The strain on these RN captains, working with inexperienced crews and unfamiliar ships, was exacerbated by the difficult waters in which they operated. In August 1916 Commander England noted that there was 'dense fog, impossible to stop any ship unless you run into her', and the following month he had a desperate near-miss. His ship was to be relieved by *Andes* and the rendezvous turned out to be in thick fog. He recorded what happened: 'We were going dead slow ahead and she suddenly appeared going about 10 knots end on. I went full speed astern and she put her helm hard aport and she cleared our stern by yards.' Later, he ironically noted that 'all the gin and whiskey is finished in the ward room, amusing in some ways'.

Calyx was a small (2,876 tons) single-screw vessel, ex-Wilson Line. She commissioned under Commander T E Wardle who left an account of how difficult the northern seas could be for such ships:

> We were westward of St Kilda and never thought we should live through it. We had only a single screw which raced as we pitched ... and I dared not go at any speed. I tried to keep her with the wind on the bow – if we had gone beam on the water would have poured down the accommodation hatches ... we were rolling 30 degrees each way and all one could do was hang on to lifelines on the bridge.

Shortly afterwards the ship was withdrawn from service as manifestly unsuitable for the task.

Sometimes the strain and stress proved too much. Commander Cecil France-Hayhurst of *Patuca*, for example, was hospitalised in Glasgow on his return to port in November 1915 and died there. The previous July, his ship had been involved in a collision in attempting to stop and board the Swedish ship *Oscar II*; the Swedish ship, a known blockade runner, sank as a result. On 26 October when patrolling south of Iceland in a southwesterly gale, both main condensers were salting. He opened them up in turn and plugged the leaky tubes without reducing speed below 10 knots and reported ready for full speed within two hours: a tricky and stressful operation in seas known to be dangerous. France-Hayhurst's brother, a lieutenant colonel in the army, also lost his life in the war, on the Western Front.

Other captains became conscious of the steady erosion of their well-being. England commented on the occasion of his fortieth birthday, 'can't shake off this 'flu or cold or whatever it is and am plagued with neuralgia,' and a little later he recorded in his diary, 'I can't sleep at night and am feeling rather worn.'

Melancholia could take over, as Commander England's diary for October 1916 shows:

> I love Margy and Bet and Puss [his children] and wish for them happiness, riches and honour, but still more the salvation of their souls and the light of truth. And I too crave the salvation of my soul and the quenching of doubt, that we may all dwell together in eternity and that all separations may be but temporary. And I who wish this am a very sinful man.

Some failed completely to deal with the stress. *Kildonan Castle* docked in Glasgow at the conclusion of her first duty on the blockade. Here, 'it was discovered that her captain, Commander Cardate, had been suffering from an excessive thirst and had the DTs'. This came to light when he sent for the Glasgow chief of police and reported that the ship was full of German and Austrian officers. He was quietly relieved on 19 December 1916 and sent to the navy's Haslar Hospital in Gosport for treatment.

The daily grind of blockade and boarding, often in appalling weather and with the ever-present threat of instant oblivion through mine or U-boat, was not what 10th Cruiser Squadron captains had trained or hoped for. But they stuck to their tasks with grim determination and mordant pride. And a little recognition went a long way. Around 28 December 1916 *Orvieto* intercepted ten ships and sent four to Kirkwall under armed guard. This brought a 'Well done' from Tupper, 'which gave much pleasure,' recorded England.

One of the stranger aspects of patrol duty was the tedious boredom of much of it, juxtaposed with the constant underlying threat of sudden death. Lieutenant Shuter's diary gives an insight into the everyday 'ordinariness' of life. He was originally posted as a PT instructor on board *Royal Arthur*, where he reported, 'there isn't a vast amount to do'. Transferred to *Endymion*, he soon had a run in with her captain, Hyde Parker; 'I don't think he likes me,' Shuter mused. Life on board followed the navy's time-worn ways; on 24 August 1914 he noted, 'Very little doing today. No gunnery drills as everyone was chipping paint. Forenoon watch. Turned in early.'

The following January he and Brocklebank were commissioning *Changuinola*, and Shuter wanted a ship's dog. On 4 January he went twice to Temple Meads dogs' home, but they were closed each time. Eventually he secured one on the following day and reported, 'finally got a Bull Terrier Bitch, a fine beast' (a strange choice as they are independent and stubborn, although good ratters). His days could be long and dull and his diary demonstrates that both on ship and shore he whiled away the hours of ennui with a lot of piano practice. Perhaps seeking more company and solace than the officers' mess could provide, he sourced a dog for himself whilst berthed in Glasgow. Shuter's diary entry for 7 April 1915 records, 'got a dog … they call him a Scotch Terrier but I believe he is a Cairn … I'm going to call him Rufus'. Three days later Commander Brocklebank returned from shore leave and brought him some French chocolates. The humdrum nature of these activities contrasts markedly with the terrifying days at sea, at risk of weather and torpedo.

Altogether forty-six captains, twenty-four with the rank of commander RN and twenty-two full captains RN, served in 10th Cruiser Squadron under the command of de Chair between 1914 and March 1916. Four died in the course of their duties. Intriguingly, so far as the author can determine, only two were promoted to flag rank during or immediately after the war and whilst on active service. For men who were commanders, this is perhaps explained by the requirement for service as a ranking captain in command of a ship; for those already holding the rank of captain, not so. Does this indicate that these were men not of the highest command quality; or was it that the squadron, once comprised derelict cruisers and then passenger liners, was simply seen by the powers-that-be as a 'second-class' navy, not suitable for training up real leaders or proving them in 'real' war?

Such a view may be supported by the squadron's various nicknames: originally the Terrible Tenth, they became the Ragtime Squadron and then, as the Elders Line banana boats started to be commissioned, the Banana Fleet, then just Bananas.*

If that were the case, it would be a vile calumny on the commitment, resolution and inner strength of this underrated and now largely forgotten body of men.

*The author wonders if this was the source of the term 'bananas' to describe someone who is considered somewhat mad.

1 2

On Patrol, 1915–1916

The Northern Patrol blockade duty was long and frequently dull: 'Life was often tedious, as much of the time spent on patrol consisted of little action.' Ships were at action stations for most of the time on patrol, lookouts and men all miserable wet and cold. As de Chair described it, 'captains and officers on the bridge peering into the darkness. Dawn breaks over a grey and stormy sea, ships rolling and pitching heavily. As the horizon lightens it is scanned by the lookouts in the crows' nests far and wide for any sign of blockade runners'.

Each cruiser had a definite area allotted to it for patrol duty, but these were changed frequently in accordance with wireless signals received from the flagship. The ships remained on their patrol stations regardless of weather, and as will readily be imagined, this was a specially trying task to crews whose lives had been mainly spent in transatlantic voyages, where exposure to bad weather had been usually limited to a few days, to be followed by the comforts of port and home. On one memorable occasion a gale sprang up which lasted for three weeks, but it brought no respite, for not a ship could leave her station except when relieved or in the discharge of duty. Off the Faroes and Iceland the temperature frequently remained below freezing point for considerable periods, and the whole of the upper deck of the ships on these stations became a mass of snow and ice, which could not be got rid of until the ship left for a lower latitude. A patrol cruise generally lasted for thirty days, more if coal supply allowed, but this was a level of endurance well beyond the old *Edgars*.

De Chair himself described the method of blockade to an American newspaper correspondent:

> A modern blockade is not a ring of ships steaming within sight of each other, forming a sort of fence across sea-tracks to enemy countries. Our North Sea blockade consists of the strategic placing of units of patrolling squadrons, all out of sight of each other but within easy steaming distance. Usually our cruisers are about twenty miles apart, and as each cruiser is afforded a clear view of fifteen miles to the horizon, no blockade runner can pass between them without being seen by one or both.

He went on to give his reason for the employment of AMCs: 'Such ships are not properly warships at all, for the superior fighting craft of the Royal Navy – superior in armament, ordnance and speed – are kept inviolate for the long-anticipated engagement which we hope to fill with the German Navy.' Still, the great new Trafalgar was awaited (ironically, the interview was published on the day of the battle of Jutland, 31 May 1916).

If an AMC came across a vessel, they would call on it to stop, usually by raising a red flag and a signal hoist. If necessary a warning shot would be fired across the bows. Once the intercepted vessel had stopped, the cruiser sent a boarding party. If it could be proved that the ship was carrying military contraband or goods bound for Germany, the offending vessel was taken as a prize, a prize crew put on board and the ship sent to a port in Britain for adjudication before a prize court. The boarding process was not without risk:

> It was at this point as a rule that the real fun began, for unless the weather made the task impossible, the ship had to be boarded by two officers. This involved the lowering of a boat and its crew, in which the officers were rowed across, whilst the cruiser stood at watchful attention to its representatives and the object of their inquiry. In fine weather the operation of boarding a ship was a matter of ease, but in heavy weather it was attended by great risk, and it is a fine tribute to the seamanship of the boat crews generally that accidents were rare.

De Chair described the process in similar terms:

> The cruiser's signals announce that an officer will be sent aboard to examine the ship's manifests. Accompanied by an armed guard of five men, the boarding officer goes over the cruiser's side, and often at some peril to life and limb manages somehow to clamber up to the tramp's deck. I have often seen the cruiser's dory stove in, and the boarding party thrown into the water.

The boarding procedure involved the cruiser positioning herself to windward or, if no wind, ahead of the target vessel. A sea boat was lowered, often a 27ft whaler. All ships were equipped with an Evinrude outboard motor for their boats, but they were not much liked or trusted by the cruiser commanding officers. The old-time, tried and trusted method of oars or sail was generally preferred, despite squadron standing orders stressing the value of the outboard engine.

If the intercepted ship was free of contraband, it was generally allowed to proceed. If suspect, it would be sent to a British harbour for examination, either under a prize crew or escorted by an armed vessel. Boarding officers had to be alert for all kinds of subterfuge: hollow masts, double bulkheads and many other disguises. Barrels of flour contained cotton for the manufacture of munitions. On one occasion a large basket of onions was observed by the boarding officer who, upon picking one out, found that it bounced over his head. It was made of rubber.

Prize Crews

As noted above, the job of the boarding crew did not just extend to inspection; often they had to sail the vessel to a British port themselves. Lieutenant Hugh D Wynne RNR was awarded the DSC for his part in such an adventure when in January 1916 he and his armed guard had to deal with a potential disaster. His citation reads: 'showed great perseverance and energy when on charge of the armed guard on board the Norwegian barque *Buccanti*'. The sailing ship had been dismasted in heavy weather and Wynne and his men managed nonetheless to get her to port and safety. His luck was not to last; he was lost along with all the crew when the submarine *E34* was sunk off the coast of Holland in 1918 and is remembered at the Noorwijk cemetery.

On a practical level, the officer and armed guard of the boarding party had to be self-sufficient in food, for they had no right to be fed or supplied on board a captive vessel. They usually took a two-day supply of tinned bully beef and bread, and tried to cadge a warm drink from the ship's galley. For defence they took revolvers, rifles, cutlasses and bandoliers of ammunition.

The duty of leading the boarding party often fell to a young midshipman. *Orvieto* received one armed guard back via *Patia* on 5 September 1916, but had five other parties away. The Norwegian *Christianafjord* was sent to Kirkwall under Mr Sutcliffe, another ship under Mr Tillotson, and a Dutch steamer under Mr Causer. 'They are gaining experience these midshipmen,' Commander England noted in his diary.

The practice of putting armed guards on board the apprehended neutral vessels, to ensure their compliance with orders to sail to British ports, exposed the boarding party to considerable risk. And their legal position was less than certain, too.

In order to get to British ports, the captured vessels had to sail through the zone in which the Germans had declared unrestricted submarine activity. As a result the prize crews were liable to come under attack whilst on board the neutral vessel. On 28 March 1915 Jellicoe issued the following rules to 10th Cruiser Squadron:

(a) The officer in charge must endeavour to arrange for the neutral ship to escape.

(b) The officer must not use the neutral ship as a weapon for attacking the submarine unless actually attacked by her.

(c) The prize crew must not fight on the deck of the neutral ship unless the submarine has committed a hostile act against the neutral ship. In the latter event the prize crew are justified in fighting to the last.

These instructions seemed to the commander-in-chief to meet the needs of the law, but it led to lengthy debate with the law officers of the Crown and the Admiralty. However, before the lawyers could come to a conclusion, the German naval attaché in Sweden announced that the Germans considered they had a full right to torpedo every neutral vessel with a prize crew on board. Jellicoe therefore applied to the Admiralty for permission to arm the boarding parties with 'lance bombs' (a 7lb charge of amatol on the end of a long stick) to enable them to fight off a submarine attacker. Predictably, this led the lawyers into further realms of vacuity, for it was considered that to initiate a hostile act such as throwing a lance bomb from the deck of the neutral ship would, in effect, be to commit an act of war under a neutral flag, an action that could undoubtedly raise serious complications with neutral states.

Eventually, common sense prevailed and it was recognised that Britain was fighting a war for the survival of everyone, including lawyers at the Foreign Office! It was decided that a guard placed on board a ship to compel the master to bring a neutral vessel into port had the same right of resistance as a prize crew which was in possession of a ship seized as a prize. However, it wasn't until 27 August that a decision was reached, causing considerable stress to the boarding parties.

The armed guards 'enjoyed' many escapades and adventures. On 28 July the Norwegian steamer *Trondhjemsfjord* was proceeding towards Kirkwall with an armed guard from *Hildebrand* on board, when a German submarine opened fire on her bows. The master altered course to put the submarine astern and a stern chase developed, in which there would only be one winner. The submarine closed the gap and after a chase of half an hour fired a second shot which stopped the steamer. The submarine then ordered the master on board with the ship's papers. Before disembarking, he and his wife disguised the armed guard and dressed the officer in charge in the skipper's old clothes, concealing their rifles and gear in the forepeak.

Subsequently, the submarine ordered 'abandon ship', and when the steamer's boats were clear torpedoed the neutral vessel. The ship sank shortly afterwards. In rare compliance with prize rules, the submarine then towed the boats for a distance of about four miles until she met the Norwegian barque *Glance*, which she ordered to embark the boats' complements. The armed guard eventually reached Thurso with no loss of life, after transfer to a trawler.

Another example of the boarding parties' picaresque lifestyle came on 23 July and involved an armed guard from *Motagua* aboard the Norwegian steamer *Fimreite* on July. About 0400 a submarine was sighted on the port bow making for the vessel at full speed. *Fimreite* hove to and the master went alongside the submarine.

The officer in charge of the guard ordered his men to remove their uniforms, dress as common sailors, and help launch the ship's boats. When *Fimreite*'s master returned, he told the guard that he had informed the German captain that there were an officer and four English sailors on board, to which the German replied, 'Don't let them go into the boats. Let them sink.'

However, the guard had already got themselves into the lifeboats with only their revolvers as arms, carried in their pockets, and after the submarine sank the Norwegian ship they were picked up and transferred safely to Stornaway.

Such luck did not always attend the boarding parties. *Pass of Balmaha*, an American full-rigged ship, was stopped on 21 July by *Victorian* and an armed guard, consisting of a sub lieutenant RNR, one petty officer and four men, put on board with orders to take her to Lerwick or Kirkwall as the wind allowed. Two days later they were intercepted by a German submarine, despite the vessel flying American ensigns, and her papers examined. The armed guard hastily changed into borrowed clothes and hid in the forepeak. The German captain ordered the American ship to Cuxhaven, put a warrant officer on board and remained alongside until relieved by another submarine, which kept in touch all the way to Heligoland. All this time the guard stayed in hiding, hoping that a British patrol would re-intercept them. They had no such fortune and on arrival at Cuxhaven on 1 August gave themselves up to become prisoners of war (it was this ship, renamed *Seeadler*, that became von Luckner's raider in the Pacific, see Chapter 7).

Young men of limited naval and life experience often found themselves called to discover their powers of leadership in testing situations. Francis Poole, a merchant marine apprentice from the northeast of England, had been accepted as a midshipman RNR in the summer of 1915 and, after an induction period at Chatham, was appointed in November to *Alcantara*. In his four months' service on her he grew up quickly. Poole was twice placed in command of the armed guard on board neutral ships ordered into a British port, and on the second of these voyages, in February 1916, he found himself trapped on a Norwegian sailing ship with a hostile master and crew for ten days, and in appalling weather. He was more than pleased to be transferred to *King Alfred*, flagship of the 9th Cruiser Squadron in the South Atlantic where he rather dismissively commented that he 'was now in the real navy'.

Death was an ever-present threat. *Orvieto* had put an armed guard of three men and a midshipman, Mr Campbell, onto a Danish sailing vessel to conduct her to Kirkwall for processing. Just off Muckle Flugga she met a German submarine. The crew and the armed guard abandoned ship in rough seas, twenty or so in the ship's boat and six in a dinghy. The dinghy overturned and the Danish mate and carpenter were drowned. Campbell was in the water for forty-five minutes before he could be pulled into the boat, and was unconscious when dragged aboard.

Another misfortune awaiting boarding parties was to discover that the Germans had got there first. In October 1916 *Otway* sighted a British steamer flying the Norwegian flag. She claimed to be SS *Older*, but a quick inspection of Lloyd's List found that ship to be in Le Havre. Captain Booty ordered the boarding party away, a midshipman and only two sailors, who were rather surprised to find that *Older*, and her valuable cargo of black coal, was in the control of a prize crew from a German submarine. Additionally, she carried as prisoners the crew of a British trawler and Italian steamship sunk by the U-boat. The Germans threatened to blow the vessel up with hidden bombs, but Booty was undeterred and forced a close boarding of the ship, transferred all men on board and eventually bought her home to port.

And sometimes the intercepted masters simply declined to play ball at all. Commander England met a Swedish ship whose captain refused point-blank to comply with the armed guard's instructions; in the end he had to put four officers and twelve men on board to physically sail her to port.

The risks involved in boarding operations were not confined to the problems of recalcitrant merchant masters or German submarines. Some were self-inflicted. As first lieutenant of *Changuinola*, John Shuter was often in charge of lowering the boarding party's boat. In April 1915 the vessel stopped to board the trawler *Ethel* and 'owing to a mistake I lowered the boat before we stopped and it capsized. Clark, Inglis and the crew were all chucked out'. Fortunately, the seas were calm and smooth and it was relatively simple to recover the unfortunate sailors. Shuter went on: 'it was an awful experience. Inglis got a chill so I kept his first watch'. That was the least he could do! In more difficult seas such a miscalculation could have cost lives.

Triumph and Tragedy

Tragedy was always a possibility for the 10th Cruiser Squadron in the freezing, dark and dangerous northern waters, and in other parts of the patrol too. On 13 January 1915 HMS *Viknor*, previously *Viking* and originally RMS *Atrato*, a beautiful, almost luxury, yacht-like liner in peacetime, built for the Royal Mail Steam Packet Company, was patrolling in heavy seas off the northwest coast of Donegal. Just by Tory Island, she hit a German mine and – unprepared for such a calamity by her builders – sank like a stone, taking all twenty-two officers and 273 crew with her. There was not even time to get off a radio message. Bodies were washed ashore for days afterwards and buried on remote Rathlin Island, Bonamargy Friary and at Ballintoy, County Antrim. Amongst the dead was her captain, Commander Ballantyne, and two brothers, Alfred and David Wright, both RNVR, aged seventeen and nineteen years respectively (see Appendix 4). The body of Commander Ernest Orford Ballantyne was washed ashore in February and was taken home, where he was buried with full military honours in Dalkieth cemetery.

Viknor had been en route for Liverpool for leave and refit, but she was carrying a very unusual cargo. Two days earlier she had intercepted *Bergensfjord*, a regular thorn in 10th Cruiser Squadron's collective side, northeast of the Faroes, where that vessel had been trying to sneak through to the north in the dark. Amongst the large number of passengers on board was one Rosato Spero, travelling on a Mexican passport, and who had been the subject of a signal to de Chair from the Admiralty. The signal had led to the admiral tasking *Viknor* and others with finding the Norwegian vessel. Spero was taken unawares in the act of burning his private papers. On hearing of the capture, de Chair sent a hasty 'Well done', and had rushed to rendezvous with *Viknor*, taking

Teutonic and *Orotava* with him. 'Spero' was none other than Count Botho von Wedel, privy councillor to the Kaiser and chief of the German spy bureau. And now, through information provided from British intelligence agents in America, he was a prisoner. *Viknor* was ordered to take on board the count and seven German stowaways, escort the prize to Kirkwall, and then to convey the prisoners to Liverpool for interrogation. When the ship went down, she took von Wedel and his knowledge of Germany's spying networks with her.

The old *Edgar*s had suffered badly in the terrible seas of the Northern Patrol area and the AMCs were a great improvement in sea-keeping qualities. But even they were not immune to the dreadful weather prevalent. On 2 February 1915 *Clan Macnaughton* (commanded by Captain Robert Jeffrey RN), patrolling to the north of Ireland, was wrecked in a gale. She sank with the loss of all 281 crew, including fifty boys straight out of the navy's shore training base at Shotley, HMS *Ganges*, and nine men from the Isle of Lewis.

Her loss has never been satisfactorily explained, but was probably the result of a combination of three factors: a terrible Atlantic gale (in her last contact she had described the weather as 'horrible'); the inexperience of her crew in handling such a ship; and the top-heavy characteristic given by the fitment of her guns. Indeed, the latter point provoked a question in the House of Commons; on 3 March Bertram Falle, MP for Portsmouth, asked 'if His Majesty's ship "Clan Macnaughton" was surveyed after her guns were put aboard; and, if so, was she passed and by what authority?' Dr MacNamara, parliamentary secretary to the Admiralty, replied that

> the 'Clan Macnaughton', a nearly new vessel of the Clan Line, classed by the British Corporation Registry, was fitted out for His Majesty's service at Tilbury under the supervision of naval, con-structive, and engineering officers deputed to act for that purpose. The armament placed in the vessel was light in comparison with her size, and all necessary stiffening to take it was fitted. Investigations as to the loading and the stability of the vessel were made at the Admiralty, and instructions were

issued to the commanding officer of the ship. The Admiralty are satisfied that the vessel was in good condition and seaworthy, and that she possessed ample stability.

This confidence was not shared by the officers of the 10th Cruiser Squadron. One officer from *Cedric* noted in his diary that

the Admiralty have been stirred to action by the criticism of Lord Charles Beresford [MP] and others upon the un-seaworthy state in which some of our Squadron have been sent to sea and have ordered the *Calyx* to pay off. We know well enough that she is unstable. The *Clan Macnaughton*'s officers were firmly convinced that nothing could save the ship from capsizing if she met really bad weather and their fears were unfortunately all too well founded. The Constructor's Department at the Admiralty ought to render up some victims for hanging after the war; it is they who have passed the ships and allowed them to go to sea with empty holds and guns on deck and nobody with the least idea how these novel conditions would affect their stability.

Submarines were a constant menace to the AMCs of 10th Cruiser Squadron. On 11 March 1915 the ex-Elders and Fyffes banana ship *Bayano* was sunk by *U-27* off the coast of Galloway. A 5,948grt vessel, she sank in only three minutes, taking 195 crewmen with her, most of whom had been asleep below. Only four officers and twenty-two men were saved. Those rescued were picked up by the Belfast collier *Balmerino*, whose captain sighted a speck on the horizon that he took to be a submarine's periscope. Drawing closer, he realised it was a raft with a sailor vigorously waving a shirt attached to an oar. Another collier, *St Katherine*, found rafts and boats which it towed in to harbour, all empty but provisioned. Captain H C Carr of *Bayano* was not amongst the survivors.

The German commander's bag might have been even greater, for after sinking *Bayano* he intercepted the AMC *Ambrose* in the Oversay Channel. Under Commander Charles W Bruton RN, *Ambrose* evaded the first two torpedoes, worked up to her maximum speed of 14 knots, and when the submarine came close to the surface to launch another attack, opened a storm of 4.7in gunfire on the German vessel which drove her off. *Ambrose* reported that she had sunk her, but it was not true.

During 1915 the Northern Patrol had been worked only by armed merchant cruisers. However, de Chair was troubled by his inability to catch Norwegian coastal vessels which headed for territorial waters and safety before he could detain them. He thought a submarine might be better suited to the purpose and it was arranged that an E-class boat be sent. This proved to be a disaster, as the boat could not stand up to the weather whilst on the surface and quickly became damaged. Something else had to be tried.

He turned to the one type of vessel that had from the outset been designed to withstand the weather of the northern latitudes – the trawler. *Tenby Castle* was sent from Scapa and soon had better success. Under the stewardship of an RNR skipper, Lieutenant J T Randell, she soon made an impact. On 30 June she sighted the German steamer *Pallas* just outside Norwegian territorial waters off Kya Island; she refused to stop till a shot was fired across her bow, and even then headed for the shore. Finally, Randell put two men on board as armed guard. Meanwhile, the *Pallas* was drawing nearer the shore and reached territorial waters. Randell's issues were made even more complicated because the boarding had been witnessed by several other vessels, including the Norwegian patrol boat, and when the Norwegian navy captain requested him to release *Pallas* he had no alternative but to comply.

But *Tenby* was soon to have her revenge. On 8 July she sighted the German steamer *Friedrich Arp* off the Huso and Haran Islands on the Norwegian coast, and having fired a shot across her bows, ordered her to steer southwest by west. The German captain ignored this order and steered towards the land. This time Randell fired a shot into the steamer's stern. That stopped the German, but she still refused to steer as ordered. Randell informed her captain that he would be sunk unless he obeyed orders. Disregarding or disbelieving this, the German vessel again made for the shore. *Tenby Castle* opened fire and sent sixteen rounds into *Friedrich Arp*'s starboard quarter and she quickly sank. The crew and pilot were rescued and transferred to *India*. The ship had been bound to Stettin from Narvik with a cargo of magnetic ore (magnetite, ferrous-ferric oxide), an essential commodity for the German war effort in a number of industrial processes.

The necessity of such a patrol in or near territorial waters became clear, and from then on trawlers were deployed in that mission, with one ship of the 10th Cruiser Squadron always within a hundred miles of them to provide support if needed. The crews of the trawlers were to cultivate friendly relations with the local fishermen and endeavour to keep their own movements and positions hidden from the enemy. Thus the humble fishing vessel joined the serried ranks of the 'misfit navy' de Chair had assembled.

On 8 August 1915 the ex-P&O steamship HMS *India* stopped off Helligvær, near Bodø, Norway, to investigate a suspected blockade runner and was torpedoed by *U-22*. She went down in five minutes taking 160 men of her crew with her. Two boatloads of survivors pulled ashore, while the remainder were picked up by the armed trawler *Saxon* and a Swedish steamer, *Gotaland*. Commander W G A Kennedy of *India* in his report stated his 'admiration at the magnificent behaviour of the officers and men, as notwithstanding the appalling swiftness of the catastrophe, the most perfect discipline prevailed until the end'.

Midshipman Ernest L McKeag RNR had joined *India* in April. As the ship went down he jumped into the water and found a mast and then a door to hang onto as a flotation aid, having gone under three times and fought his way back to the surface on each occasion. In the cold water, the symptoms of exposure soon set in. 'I was fearfully cold,' he recorded in his diary, 'I felt very sleepy; a piece of wood wedged itself between myself and the mast and I rested my chin on it and knew no more … when I came to I was surprised to find myself huddled in the bottom of a boat that was alongside the *Gotaland*.'

In the morning he 'woke up to discover that I was dressed in shirt and underpants belonging to the captain of the vessel', and learned that he had been the last survivor to be picked up, having been in the water for three hours. He was very lucky to be alive.

The Swedish vessel proceeded to port in Narvik, followed by Kennedy in *Saxon*. The Norwegian authorities were quite willing to let *Saxon* go to sea again with all she had saved. But as there was no food or accommodation and everyone was worn out, reluctantly Commander Kennedy decided upon internment, committing the survivors to sit out the war. Under international law, those rescued by *Gotaland* were not classed as internees as they had been landed from a neutral vessel. After a short delay they were allowed to return to England.

The Norwegians had treated all the men well and on 12 August held a bilingual service of remembrance for the twelve men, all RNR or RFR, who had been dead on arrival in port or washed ashore. They sang two Norwegian hymns and 'Nearer My God to Thee'. There is a common grave and memorial at Bodø.

International considerations also impinged on de Chair's command. On 5 November 1915 the American government, in one of its periodic fits of moralising, delivered a protest against the blockade in stronger terms than they had hitherto used. By way of defending against such accusation, to demonstrate that the blockade was an international and not just British affair, and that 'the doctrine of legitimate restriction of neutral trade upon which we were acting was not confined to ourselves', the French were enjoined into the Northern Patrol.

However, France offered only an unsuitable ship for the purpose, so it was arranged that one of the 10th Cruiser Squadron should be transferred to her flag. *Digby* (an ex-Furness Withy passenger and cargo liner) was accordingly sent down to Brest, and after receiving a French crew and commission, rejoined the squadron as *Artois*. The French decided that they should make a further contribution and so another ship, *Oropesa*, an old (1895) Royal Mail Pacific Steam and Navigation liner, was handed over in the same way. She was rechristened *Champagne*, but retained her British crew and worked under de Chair's aegis, but not command, as a monthly packet ship between France and Archangel in Russia (on rejoining 10th Cruiser Squadron command, she was sunk by a submarine in the Irish Sea on 9 October 1917, with the loss of fifty-six men).

American moralising did not, of course, prevent them making good money out of the sufferings of war. McKeag, now in the *Orotava,* and having survived a hurricane-force storm which required them to return to Glasgow for repairs, recorded that on their next patrol they intercepted an American ship carrying 'aeroplanes and armoured cars for the Germans'.

The strain of the command, de Chair's less than forceful manner, and the continued leakage of ships and trade through the blockade (such as *Moewe*), led some at the Admiralty to consider replacing him. First Sea Lord, Sir Henry B Jackson, broached with Admiral Jellicoe (then Commander-in-Chief, Grand Fleet but a friend of de Chair from their time working together in the Third Sea Lord's office) the possibility of de Chair being appointed Senior Naval Officer and Admiral Superintendent of Gibraltar Dockyard (a largely administrative and undemanding post). On 23 July 1915 Jellicoe wrote to Jackson:

> I should very much doubt de Chair's liking Gibraltar. It would – if precedents go for anything – be fatal to his future. He is a very first rate sea officer & is suited to any command afloat. I should doubt his caring to leave 10th CS for anything but a sea command and I should be very sorry to see him placed in a position which might prejudice his future. I do not want to suggest that he should not leave 10th CS if the winter is expected to try him too highly, but only to beg that if he goes it may be to a sea command.

At sea the 10th Cruiser Squadron, in common with all Britain's serving men, faced constant danger but, unbelievably perhaps, industrial unrest and labour troubles continued on shore and par-ticularly at Liverpool, de Chair's bête noire of 1914. He was further outraged to discover on 28 December that his vessels in the Clyde (for repair and maintenance) could not sail on account of the workmen's Christmas holidays. Jellicoe wrote to the Admiralty on de Chair's behalf, but the reply was that nothing could be done. It seems difficult, at today's distance, to comprehend what exactly it was about the life or death struggle that the country was engaged in that was not comprehensible to these shore-based workers. The recalcitrant attitude and unpatriotic greed shown by some of the dockyard workers riled the serving sailors, and things had not improved by 1917 when Captain England was incensed after his ship put into port for re-provisioning:

> The enormous wages we have seen seem so unfair. Thus each labourer who coaled this ship at Newcastle received £17 for a week's work and it is the same scale in all the shipyards.

Meanwhile the volunteer fighter dies on his soldier's pay. If this is democracy then the Germans are right sticking to their Kaiser.

*   *   *

From 24 December 1914 to 5 May 1915 the armed merchant cruisers had boarded and examined 926 vessels and had sent in 258 of these with armed guards. Between 7 March and 19 April 1915 (forty-four days) they had intercepted 364 vessels, including fishing craft. The total number of merchant ships which passed through from one neutral port to another without being intercepted was twenty eastbound and twenty-six westbound; and of these only three were vessels whose arrest was particularly desired. For the year of 1915, the 'worst offenders' were the Norwegians and the Danes; of 2,495 ships intercepted, 1,463 came from these two countries and of 742 sent in, 608 were from these so-called neutrals.

On 1 January 1916 de Chair was appointed an Additional Member of the Second Class, or Knight Commander, in the Military Division of the Most Honourable Order of the Bath (KCB) – in other words, he became 'Sir Dudley'. Beatty, commanding the Battle Cruiser Fleet, was fulsome in his praise for his quondam successor as naval secretary: 'yours has been a great work and no one but yourself can understand or know how arduous and responsible it has been,' he wrote. But eventually the Admiralty got their way, and Jellicoe's blandishments were ignored, for on 6 March de Chair struck his flag and was superseded in command of the 10th Cruiser Squadron. The very same day he was appointed naval adviser to the Foreign Office Minister of Blockade (Restriction of Enemy Supplies Department) Lord Robert Cecil, in matters concerning enemy trade.

De Chair was never in doubt as to the success his squadron had achieved, however. Writing to the Admiralty in 1915 he stated that:

the officers and men under my orders would, I know, far rather serve in men-of-war designed to fight those of the enemy; yet they have without exception cheerfully carried out their duties … That these duties had their dangers was shown by the fact that 80 officers and 1,185 men of the squadron had been lost, all of whom died in the performance of their duty.

The armoured cruiser HMS *Achilles*, which sank the German auxiliary cruiser *Leopard* in March 2017. (AUTHOR'S COLLECTION)

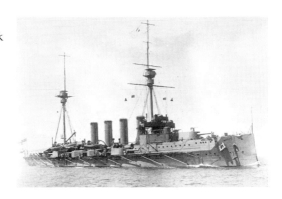

Rear Admiral Sydney Fremantle on patrol. (AUTHOR'S COLLECTION)

The memorial in Bodo, Norway, to the dead of HMS *India*. (AUTHOR'S COLLECTION)

Changuinola in pre-war days. (AMBROSE GREENWAY COLLECTION)

A 1933 photograph
of Admiral Sir
Dudley de Chair.
(The National
Portrait Gallery)

Orvieto
before the war.
(Ambrose Greenway
collection)

Above: A view of Busta Voe, where the 10th lay at anchor, taken around 1914 and showing the bleak, windswept landscape. (SHETLAND MUSEUM AND ARCHIVES)

Below: The Hillswick Hotel, photographed c1914, which de Chair took over as an officers' mess. (SHETLAND MUSEUM AND ARCHIVES)

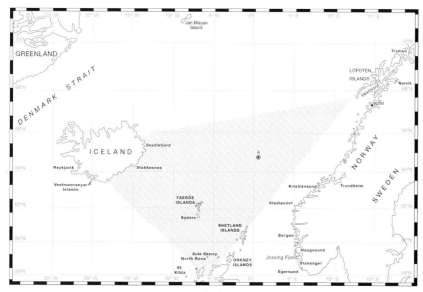

Area patrolled by the Blockaders

A map showing the basic operating areas of the Northern Patrol. Point A marks the place of encounter between *Achilles*, *Dundee* and *Leopard*. (SUE CAMERON)

HMS *Changuinola* in the dazzle paint which the 10th Cruiser Squadron adopted during 1916. (AUTHOR'S COLLECTION)

RMS *Cedric* in peacetime. (AMBROSE GREENWAY COLLECTION)

Cap Trafalgar is sunk by *Carmania* off Trinidad, September 1914.
Painting by Charles Dixon.
(© NATIONAL MARITIME MUSEUM, GREENWICH, LONDON, PT2974)

Detail of a painting by John Everett depicting a dazzle-painted merchant ship on the Thames. Another artist, Norman Wilkinson, was credited with the early development of dazzle camouflage.
(© NATIONAL MARITIME MUSEUM, GREENWICH, LONDON, PY6702)

The 4.7in guns mounted on the foredeck of an armed merchant cruiser. (AUTHOR'S COLLECTION)

Two photographs of *Bayano*, built in 1913 by Alexander Stephen & Son, Glasgow, showing her as built and, later, as HMS *Bayano*, coverted to an armed merchant cruiser. She was intercepted and sunk northwest of Corsewall Point, Portpatrick, by *U-27*, and her captain, H C Carr, and 181 ratings were lost. (AMBROSE GREENWAY COLLECTION)

The Long Duty Ends, 1916–1917

De Chair's replacement was Vice Admiral Reginald Godfrey Otway Tupper, previously Rear Admiral Orkneys, a shore-based appointment. He was five years de Chair's senior and an old-fashioned sailor in all respects who, in his twenties, had written an article for the *RUSI Journal* arguing that there was no benefit to be gained by appointing naval officers through meritocratic competitive examination, as recruiting from the sons of officers and gentlemen would provide 'brains sufficient to satisfy the scientific requirements of the Service'.

Also in March 1916 Jellicoe, concerned that the squadron was inadequate for the task in hand, and stung by the successful first exit, cruise and return of *Moewe,* ordered that the Northern Patrol should be reinforced from the three Grand Fleet cruiser squadrons that he kept with him at Scapa Flow. His intention was to make it more difficult for the ingress and exit of raiders by having one cruiser watching the meridian of the Shetlands between latitude 62° and 65°, which is where he considered the raiders would have to appear. Over the course of time, this extra patrol became a supplement to the AMCs and its maintenance fell onto the shoulders of the 2nd Cruiser Squadron, which comprised the armoured (or first-class) cruisers *Minotaur* (flag), *Shannon*, *Achilles*, *Cochrane* and *Duke of Edinburgh*.

Tupper continued in much the same vein as de Chair, although he suffered an increased erosion of his forces through frequent requests to supply cruisers for other tasks and to other commands. His sole innovation seemed to be the provision of dazzle paint camouflage to his squadron, starting with his flagship *Alsatian* in August 1917.

Alsatian was actually the very first RN vessel to use dazzle camouflage, also known as 'razzle dazzle' or dazzle painting. It was a camouflage paint scheme credited to the marine artist Norman Wilkinson, then a lieutenant commander in the RNVR, and consisted of a complex pattern of geometric shapes in contrasting colours, interrupting and intersecting each other. The idea of dazzle was not to conceal the ship, but made it difficult for the enemy to estimate its type, size, speed and heading by disrupting the visual rangefinders used for naval artillery. German rangefinders were based on the co-incidence principle with an optical mechanism, operated by a human to compute the range. The operator adjusted the mechanism until two half-images of the target lined up in a complete picture. Dazzle was intended to make that hard, because clashing patterns looked abnormal even when the two halves were aligned. As an additional feature, the dazzle pattern usually included a false bow wave intended to make estimation of the ship's speed difficult.

Eventually, around two thousand ships were so painted, supervised by the English Vorticist artist Edward Wadsworth (another RNVR officer) whose post-war canvases would celebrate his designs, as exampled by his *Dazzle Ships in Dry Dock* (National Gallery of Canada) of 1919.

Not every skipper was delighted by the schemes, however. In his diary, Sir Stephen King-Hall tells of a captain who complained to the camouflage officer that his ship had been ruined. The camouflage officer wrote in reply: 'Dear Sir, The object of camouflage is not, as you suggest, to turn your ship into an imitation of a West African parrot, a rainbow in a naval pantomime, or a "gay woman". The object of camouflage is rather to give the impression that your head is where your stern really is.'

However, the loss of ships continued. *Avenger* had been launched in 1915 as *Aotearoa* for the Union Steamship Company, New Zealand, but was requisitioned and completed as HMS *Avenger* and was commissioned in March 1916. She had been intended for the New Zealand–Vancouver run and at 15,200 tons with twin steam turbines she was a big, fast ship. She was torpedoed west of the Shetlands by *U-69* on 14 June. Loss of life was minimal, only one man being killed and one injured. Her engineering officers were all from New Zealand, having gone out to commission her into civilian life and had stayed on when she was converted.

Hilary had just completed her patrol off the Shetland Islands, and on 25 May 1917 was returning to Swarbacks Minn to coal when she was attacked and sunk by *U-88*, forty miles west of Lerwick. Fortune smiled on the crew on this occasion, for out of a total of thirty-two officers and 220 men, only four lives were lost. Her two identical sister-ships, which remained in the merchant fleet, were also sunk by submarines.

And 10th Cruiser Squadron suffered a final loss before disbandment the following month. *Otway* had been taken into the navy in November 1914, leased from the Orient Line, and joined the 10th Cruiser Squadron immediately after fitting out. She paid the price of service on 22 July 1917 when, patrolling in the Minches, she was torpedoed by the German submarine *UC-49* and sank. The crew included thirty-eight men from the Isle of Lewis, six of whom, with four of their fellow crewmen, were lost out of a complement of 349.

Some unfortunate sailors did not need to be at sea to die, and met prosaic deaths in the midst of carnage. *Alsatian*'s log reveals that on 25 March 1917 the police reported to the ship that the body of Able Seaman Truscote RNR had been found in No 1 Canada Dock, Liverpool (the ship was in dry dock there at the time). A court of inquiry into his death was convened on 28 March and his funeral held two days later at Anfield Cemetery. He was a Newfoundland man, thirty-three years old and far from home.

Finally, quondam 10th Cruiser Squadron vessels *Moldavia* and *Patia* were also lost to U-boats in the English and Bristol Channels respectively, but by then the 10th Cruiser Squadron did not exist and they were serving with other groupings. Overall, given the tasks that they were undertaking, the losses of men in the squadron might be considered surprisingly small.

*　　*　　*

On 1 February 1917 Germany resumed unrestricted submarine warfare, a strategy aimed at knocking Britain out of the war before the Americans could arrive in Europe in force. America declared war on 6 April and with that act substantially reduced the utility of the 10th Cruiser Squadron's activities. The USA and the northern neutrals had been the major source of contraband. Trade with Germany by the latter had largely been controlled by diplomatic means and treaties; now the former was an ally and any ship departing the USA was inspected at source. The issue was not now ships trying to break in through the blockade but armed vessels – raiders – trying to break out. In preventing this, the squadron had never been very successful.

The need to provide transatlantic escorts for the ships sailing from the newly allied USA to Europe, together with the belated introduction of merchant vessel convoy (see Chapter 20) saw the AMCs of 10th Cruiser Squadron progressively withdrawn to act as ocean escorts from April 1917. Tupper's command was reduced and he asked of the Admiralty whether those now in the Atlantic on detached duty still belonged to his operational command. Perhaps seeing his post endangered, he sent to the Admiralty proposals for re-tasking his squadron, including the fitting of his flagship *Alsatian* with an aircraft, demonstrating his interest in air reconnaissance.

But his, and the squadron's, fate had already been determined. At Scapa Flow on 27 July, and unbeknown to Tupper, Beatty and the planners decided that the squadron should be reduced, facilitating the transfer of more to escort duty. Further reductions soon followed and to maintain the appearance of a large squadron still *in situ,* some of the trawlers were used to generate spurious signal traffic. And on 29 November 1917, by which time only *Alsatian*, *Teutonic* and *Orvieto* had been left on patrol, the rest being out convoying, the Admiralty withdrew its tasking and broke the squadron up.

During its time of service, the 10th Cruiser Squadron had boarded 12,979 vessels, had caused 2,039 ships to go voluntarily to a UK port, and had failed to intercept 642 contraband-carrying vessels. Nine AMCs were lost during the period of patrol.

As First Lord of the Admiralty Eric Geddes commented, 'the blockade was exercised by a little advertised power, the 10th Cruiser Squadron. That squadron for 1914–18 held the 800-mile stretch of grey sea from the Orkneys to Iceland … If anything more strikingly demonstrating the value of sea power can be given, I do not know of it'.

1 4

Blockade and Trade

The British blockade was designed to deny food and essential raw materials to the enemy and only secondarily to prevent the exit and ingress of German warships or raiders. De Chair described the activities thus:

Blockade work is unspectacular, uninspiring, but exceedingly dangerous. The work of officers and men under my command has been consistently faithful and effective, under conditions which have always held the possibility, for twenty-four hours a day, of destruction by German mines and German torpedoes. The basis of that blockade rests upon the ability and courage of reserve officers and men drawn from Great Britain's Mercantile Marine. Our effort has been purely to prevent goods from reaching the enemy, never to embarrass or inconvenience neutrals of whatever nationality, who are endeavouring, under conditions of extreme difficulty, to maintain legitimate trade relations necessary to their welfare and prosperity.

Churchill, First Lord of the Admiralty at the outbreak of war, had clearly stated Britain's blockade strategy. It was to 'starve the whole [enemy] population – men, women, and children, old and young, wounded and sound – into submission'. And an American writer has noted:

the War Orders given by the Admiralty on 26 August 1914 were clear enough. All food consigned to Germany through neutral ports was to be captured and all food consigned to Rotterdam was to be presumed consigned to Germany … The British were determined on the starvation policy, whether or not it was lawful.

But the reality was much more nuanced. The whole issue of blockade was covered by international treaty and Britain needed to maintain good relations with both the USA and other neutrals, particularly the so-called 'northern neutrals' – the Scandinavians, Denmark and Holland – for reasons of both necessary reciprocal trade and as potential future fighting allies.

Germany likewise was determined to destroy British trade and shipping. As Admiral Holtzendorf (head of the German naval staff) wrote in a memorandum of 22 December 1916, 'our enemies France and Italy are economically on their knees so that they are only upheld by English energy and activity … England's mainstay is her shipping'.

The reason for the critical nature of trade was that both nations were net importers of foodstuffs and raw materials essential for the manufacture of armaments. In Britain, the repeal of the Corn Laws and subsequent flood of cheaper American and Canadian corn into the country had deterred farmers from cereal agriculture. Britain had become highly dependent on imported food supplies. During the five-year period 1909–1913, imports had accounted for 78.7 per cent of wheat and flour consumed in Britain and 56.2 per cent of cereals and pulses overall. British agriculture had responded by specialising in meat and dairy produce, but even here imports still accounted for 35.7 per cent of meat, 43.4 per cent of butter and 74.2 per cent of cheese consumption.

Indeed, in 1913 Britain imported 18.1 million tons of foodstuffs. By 1918 this had reduced to 11.4 million as a result of a focus on increasing the productivity of domestic agriculture. Between 1916 and 1918, as a consequence of strenuous efforts resultant from government policy, 7.5 million acres of British pasture land was turned over to arable. Although this led to a drop in meat production, cereal and potato yields grew by 40 per cent against peacetime levels and the calorific value of production was enhanced.

German's industrialisation, forced through with Teutonic vigour, had neglected agricultural productivity as an essential to keeping a denuded countryside at increasing levels of agricultural output. By 1914, for example, the German population was reliant on imports for 19 per cent of the calories it consumed. Over 40 per cent of protein utilised and 42 per cent of fats came from abroad. Additionally, Germany had, unlike Britain, followed a protectionist agricultural policy which sheltered its farmers from market forces and gave them little incentive to improve either efficiency or output. As a consequence, its farming industry was unable to respond to the challenge of war conditions, and rationing of bread was introduced by June 1915, with other commodities swiftly following.

Legality

As has been noted (*vide supra*), Britain ignored the Treaty of Paris when it determined in 1913 that its strategy against Germany would henceforth be based on a distant blockade. The nature of the blockade then further changed, again in contravention of the 1856 agreement, when on 3 November 1914 Britain announced, in response to the discovery of a German ship unloading mines off the English coast, that the whole of the North Sea was to be designated a military area, which would be mined and into which neutral ships proceeded 'at their own peril'. Similar measures in regard to the English Channel ensured that neutral ships would be forced to put into British ports for sailing instructions or to take on British pilots. During this time they could easily be searched as well.

The House of Lords had refused its consent to the 1909 Declaration of London, which consequently was never considered binding by Britain. This was fortuitous, for under its provisions, Britain's blanket interception of food supplies bound for Germany would have been of doubtful legal validity. As it was, the United States insisted that the belligerent nations fighting in the First World War abide by the declaration. Both the British and Germans ignored it.

American patience started to wear thin towards the end of 1914. To begin with they cloaked their demands for the freedom of the seas in the language of the impact on American trade. At the end of

December 1914 the American ambassador to the Court of St James, Walter Hines Page, was instructed to deliver a note prepared by Secretary of State William Jennings Bryan, but given its final polish by President Wilson himself. In this note, the British government was asked to make such arrangements as will 'discourage the search of ships without evidence and seizure on suspicion'. The communication went on to suggest that American industry was suffering as a result of the policy, as exporters were reluctant to ship goods that may be detained or forfeit, and stated that America viewed with concern the detention of scores of American cargoes conveyed to neutral ports.

Immediately before the delivery of the note, the influential German-American lobby in Washington had been making strong representations to President Wilson that the United States needed to act or else he would face a backlash in the forthcoming elections. As the delivery of the communication became public, the German-American supporting newspapers wrote triumphantly of the event.

Sir Edward Grey replied to Page on 7 January in the form of a holding letter making some 'preliminary observations'. He pointed out that American trade did not appear to have been adversely affected by anything, let alone blockade. Exports to Denmark in November 1914 were up 1,200 per cent compared with the prior year in dollar value, to Sweden 758 per cent and to Norway 485 per cent. However, he stressed the desire of His Majesty's Government to have strong and friendly relations with America.

The attitude of America, and the British government's wish to give no offence to its executive, explains in part the somewhat cautious nature of the operation of the blockade. As de Chair described it:

> Our boarding officer interviews the captain of the merchantman, who states his port of origin, his destination, his cargo, the length of his voyage, and whether or not he stands in need of any assistance. The crew is sometimes mustered in suspicious cases to determine whether any German subjects are aboard. Finally, the manifests are carefully examined. In many cases the neutral ship is quite innocent and is allowed immediately to proceed; in fact, whenever there is fair doubt about the cargo, we

are lenient in releasing our temporary capture. In the case of fishing trawlers, which swarm the North Sea, it is possible to examine the cargo immediately, and where ships are partly in ballast the examination may also be done quickly.

He went on to describe what happened to the peccant:

Whenever a ship is discovered to be carrying contraband an officer and an armed guard of five men are put aboard to conduct the blockade runner into our nearest port, where examination usually takes from two to five days, according to the disposition of the cargo and the consequent difficulty of removing it.

De Chair was also concerned that neutral shipping should not feel hard done by:

British Admiralty orders were issued at the very commence-ment of hostilities to the effect that all officers and men of the Royal Navy engaged in blockade work were to treat the captains and crews of suspected neutral ships with the greatest possible courtesy and consideration and to place the neutral in as little danger or inconvenience as was consistent with the proper maintenance of our blockade.

In fact, the day-to-day strategic control of the blockade came from the Foreign Office, much to the irritation of the Admiralty, who felt that the FO were too lenient in what was and wasn't permitted and which nations should be considered suspect. Many in the Admiralty thought the FO more concerned to keep neutrals 'sweet' than to prevent contraband. De Chair was certainly of that view. By October 1914 twenty-five ships had been sent into Kirkwall, but only one detained and another forced to land its cargo. De Chair complained to Jellicoe, who complained to the Admiralty, that it was all a waste of time, but the Admiralty assured them that their endeavours were having an impact. When finally an Order in Council was promulgated on 11 March 1915, which prohibited any neutral vessel to proceed to or from a German port with any goods whatsoever (and abolishing the distinction between absolute and conditional contraband), de Chair noted that, although it would increase his squadron's work load, 'many lives would have been spared and much danger to ships avoided, had this been in force at the beginning of the war … the Foreign Office were so undecided and afraid of hurting the neutrals supposed feelings'.

De Chair was further incensed by the attitude of the civil servants at the Foreign Office when he discovered, via Jellicoe, that a reserve officer and sixteen other Germans of military age had succeeded in reaching Christiania in Norway by the use of false passports, sailing on the Norwegian steamer *Bergensfjord*, despite her having been boarded by *Otway* on 29 March 1915 and sent into Kirkwall with a prize crew. De Chair rightly asked why the passengers had not been inspected as well as the cargo.

Bergensfjord had form, as it had twice previously been sent into Kirkwall and had each time attempted to evade the AMCs of the Northern Patrol. Amazingly, her captain pushed his luck again, for she was once more intercepted, by *Motagua*, and sent to harbour on 20 June, en route from New York to Bergen. On this occasion she was found to have on board 473 passengers, including two German naval officers, seven German women, and the notorious propagandist Dr Dernburg (Dr Bernhard Dernburg, the former German Imperial Secretary of State for the Colonies, who was based in the United States and represented German viewpoints in the propaganda campaign against Britain). Her cargo was general, but mostly of a suspicious nature. This time she was not allowed to proceed, although Dernburg was later allowed on his way.

On another occasion, when the American-flagged *Greenbriar* had been stopped, sent to Kirkwall full of contraband and German sailors, but then released and allowed to proceed to Bremen because the FO were afraid of the American government's reaction, de Chair commented that 'all our work and efforts in the face of extremely trying conditions [are] being thrown away by the action of some enemy sympathizer or a fat civil servant seated in safety in Downing Street'.

Some thought that the American attitude might spill over into outright hostility. Indeed, so concerned was Jellicoe in early 1916 over the American attitude to the British blockade that he considered the strategic possibility that America might enter the war against Britain. The Americans had set up a naval board to report on the question of whether or not it was necessary to send ships into British harbours for inspection, and it reported that there was no justification for such an action and that ships could be inspected at sea. When this report was passed to Jellicoe, he violently protested that this would expose his vessels to submarine attack, being stationary during the examination, to an unacceptable degree. He had further been informed by the Foreign Office and by the American ambassador, Page, that relations between the two countries were severely strained over blockade. After the war, Jellicoe cited this as one of the reasons for exercising caution in the risks that the Grand Fleet was exposed to at Jutland, for fear of having a reduced fleet to combat any American incursions.

Prize Courts and Prize Money

Neutral ships seized in the blockade were sent to the nearest port with a prize court. A prize court was a court authorised by statute to consider whether or not a ship had been lawfully captured or seized in time of war. The court could order the sale or destruction of the seized ship and the distribution of any proceeds to the captain and crew of the seizing ship. A prize court could also order the return of a seized ship to its owners if the seizure was found to be unlawful.

A High Court of Admiralty had existed in England since 1340, initially constituted to consider matters of spoil and piracy. Soon after the restoration in 1660, the business of the court divided into an instance court and a prize court. The criminal side passed to the Central Criminal Court in 1834, and when the Supreme Court of Judicature was established in 1875 the civil law business of the court joined the other civil law courts in the creation of the Probate, Divorce and Admiralty Division of the High Court of Justice. The business of the High Court of Admiralty, aside from the criminal cases above, was administered under civil law and divided into prize jurisdiction and instance jurisdiction (commercial disputes, disputes over wages, collisions, pilotage, salvage and droits). The Prize Court ruled on prize cases and either condemned the ship, cargo or both as lawful prize, or found in favour of the owners of the prize as 'not lawful prize'.

As well as determining the lawful nature of the capture or not, the courts ruled on the award of prize money. Captains and crews of HM ships capturing a prize or sinking an enemy were entitled to a share in the value of the ship and/or its cargo. This system had been in existence since the sixteenth century and had propelled many a captain or admiral up the financial ladder.

Originally, all captured ships were the property of the Crown and to ensure that its sailors displayed the necessary elan, the Crown increasingly passed on some or all of the value of the capture to the crew. Eventually, this practice was formalised via the Cruisers and Convoys Act of 1708. If the prize were an enemy merchantman, the prize money came from the sale of both ship and cargo. For a warship, if repairable, the Crown bought it at a fair price. The Crown also paid 'head money' of £5 each for captured sailors, which meant that crews much preferred to board an enemy vessel than sink her. Crewmen could make a year's money for a few hours' fighting (although there was, it should be noted, always the risk to the participant of death or capture). All ships in sight of a capture shared in the prize money, as their presence was judged to encourage the enemy to surrender without fighting until sunk.

All ranks benefitted from the prize system. Allocation was by eighths. Two-eighths of the prize money went to the captain. One-eighth of the money went to the admiral or commander-in-chief who signed the ship's written orders (unless the orders came directly from the Admiralty, in which case this eighth also went to the captain). One-eighth was divided among the lieutenants, sailing master, and captain of Marines if any. One-eighth was divided among the wardroom warrant officers (even including the chaplain!), standing warrant officers, lieutenant of Marines, and the master's mates. One eighth was divided among the junior warrant and petty officers, their mates, sergeants of Marines, captain's clerk, surgeon's mates, and midshipmen. The final two-eighths were divided among the crew, with able and specialist seamen receiving larger shares than ordinary seamen and boys.

By 1914, sinking of enemy warships was more likely than capture, given the advances in weaponry, but the system still pertained. When *Highflyer* sank *Kaiser Wilhelm der Grosse*, a prize award was made in July 1916 of £2,680 (£270,000 in today's money). Captain Buller's share would be at least £640 (today £64,000). *Carmania* received £2,115 for vanquishing *Cap Trafalgar*. On the other hand, the reluctance (as perceived by the sailors concerned) of the power-that-be to detain as prizes all the ships that were sent in by 10th Cruiser Squadron aggravated the crews and captains, not just from a professional, but also from a financial, perspective. Their harsh and demanding patrol duty made arduous physical demands which they expected to be ameliorated by a substantial booty of prize money. In their view they were being robbed by the powers-that-be when ships were released after being intercepted and sent or taken to a British port.

Nonetheless, the awarding of prize money and its distribution continued unchanged throughout the war until August 1918, when the Naval Prize Act changed the system such that the prize money was paid into a common fund from which a payment was made to all naval personnel, whether or not they were involved in an action. So, whilst the work of trade protection and blockade might be dull and largely uneventful, eventually there were considerable benefits available for prosecuting it successfully. Patriotism had its rewards!

The Northern Neutrals

The extent of the materials passing through the Scandinavian neutrals was a shock to British governmental thinking at the beginning of the war. As H W Carless Davis, the vice chair of the British War Trade Intelligence Department, noted, 'the possibility that the enemy would make use of Scandinavian ports was not fully considered. It was expected that the expense of sending goods to Germany by this circuitous route and the inadequacy of transport services between Scandinavia and Germany would confine traffic within narrow limits'. It took time to develop strategies to cope with this unforeseen development.

But by mid-war, Britain's attitude to the 'northern neutrals' can be ascertained from a memorandum prepared by the Foreign Office for the War Cabinet and considered at a meeting of that body on 1 January 1917.

It demonstrates that through a combination of negotiation, bribery, reciprocal trade and enforceable treaties, the FO (under two of Britain's most intellectually supple secretaries of state, Grey and Balfour) was managing to control the 'leakage' of food and materials into Germany from neutral countries to the point where 'with some minor exceptions, practically no goods coming from overseas are getting through to Germany'. The author of the memorandum was particularly aggrieved with the French who, unbelievably, given the ravaging of their country and armies, were still selling wines and spirits to Germany ('we have had a good deal of difficulty with the French' – *plus ça change*); and there were quibbles regarding Sweden, Norway and Denmark. For the Danes, it was recognised that they were in an invidious position for, if they wished, the Germans could easily invade their small country – given the limited forces that could be ranged against them – and take what they wanted. Nevertheless, the document asserts that 'the fact has been made full use of by the Danes and they have contrived out of their military weakness to make very large commercial profits'. However, now that the Danish perceived that Germany would not win a walkover war, 'they have modified their attitude', and the writer was hopeful of progress. Denmark's food imports before the war had totalled 187 million kroner per annum; the value for 1915 was 487 million.

With regard to Norway, Denmark and Holland, agreements were eventually signed which limited the amount of imports of military value, including food, into those countries. This thus made re-export to Germany less likely, as the goods were required for domestic consumption with little or no surplus obtaining. In some circumstances, purchasing agreements were entered into whereby the Allied powers contracted to buy all surplus production to prevent it going to the enemy. As an example, Britain regularly purchased Norwegian herring which it did not need and which was left to rot. And, of course, the absolute amounts of goods destined for neutral ports could be monitored to some extent by the blockading and boarding activities. Holland was a particular problem because, pre-war, much of Germany's incoming trade arrived via Rotterdam through Holland's inland waterways on enormous barges known as *Rheinschiffe*, and Holland was very susceptible to easy invasion and subjugation by the German army. As early as 26 August 1914 the navy had been instructed to regard all goods consigned to Rotterdam as being intended for Germany unless proved otherwise, but a delicate balancing act had to be maintained to prevent provoking a possible German attempt on Holland itself.

Britain had yet to fully get its domestic markets under control. Three months into the war it was reported that, 'Germany has been buying crossbred wool on Bradford through neutral markets, principally Holland and Sweden ... money has been forwarded directly invoices were tendered.' Cash on the nail clearly attracted the Bradford merchants, irrespective of its source. The reports went on to note that 'wool markets ... have completely sold out. Never before in the history of the wool trade ... has such a thing occurred'.

Sweden was a difficult case, not least as its king had German leanings (his mother and wife were German-born) and so did at least half of the population as a whole, who were also largely anti-Russian ('the Swedes are hostile to us,' thought Commander England); and Sweden was important as a supply route for that same rapidly failing Allied partner. Agreements had been signed only for cotton and lubricating oil, but an attempt was being made to restrict Swedish imports of other commodities through blockade by pegging their totals to a percentage of pre-war levels. This was fine for goods coming from the British Empire but under international law Britain had no right to interfere with imports from other neutral countries, such as the USA (unless it could be definitively shown that the goods were bound for Germany eventually).

The largest source of contraband to Germany's neighbours and trading partners was, of course, the USA, and as other sources of trade to Germany were indicted, American shipments increased. For example, American exports to Holland, Sweden, Norway and Denmark, which in March 1914 had totalled £1,258,000, grew by over 400 per cent to £5,098,000 in March of the following year.

This problem was being resolved with help from the American government (still at this stage neutral) under a system of 'navicerts', whereby a shipper from the USA could apply to the British Washington embassy to ascertain whether a particular consignment would have difficulty getting through the patrols. The embassy would make inquiries of the authorities in London, and if approval was given a certificate was issued. This system was not infallible, as many shippers failed to avail themselves of it, as did the South Americans; but without a navicert there was a finite risk that their vessels would be impounded by the naval patrols and sent to a British prize court for arbitration – which could take some time and might end in forfeiture.

The Impact of Blockade

The stranglehold took effect quickly. By October 1914 the Germans had already been forced to resort to rationing and adulteration. An order was passed late in the month to adulterate wholemeal flour with 10 per cent rye, on top of a previously decreed addition of 20 per cent potato flour to all bakers' products – a 30 per cent adulteration in total.

The *Daily Telegraph* on 30 October quoted the *Norddeutsche Allgemeine Zeitung*, which generally reported the views of the state, as saying that: 'Germany really has enough bread and corn for the army and people until the next harvest but the country must be thrifty in the matter of food so that after the next harvest the stocks may still be sufficient.'

But these measures proved inadequate. On 1 February 1915 the Federal Council for Germany issued an edict effectively nationalising all stocks of flour, wheat and rye. Traders were forbidden from operating on their own account. Such measures had already been put into effect in Hungary. Additionally, the German government made local municipalities responsible for securing stocks of cured meats and rationing them out appropriately.

By 1915, German imports had fallen by 55 per cent from pre-war levels. Apart from causing shortages in important raw materials such as coal and various non-ferrous metals, the blockade cut off nitrate supplies (previously obtained from Chile) that were vital to German agriculture as fertiliser and to its armaments industry for the production of explosives. One side effect was to hothouse industrial innovation. The Haber process for the synthesis of ammonia, which replaced the need for imported nitrates, was one such result.

Blockade of German imports was much more successful than Germany's early attempts on Britain's supply chain. Between 1916 and 1917, German imports of grain fell from 20,063 metric tonnes per month to 3,089; meat from 5,778 to 1,848; fish from 17,573 to 5,416; and butter from 7,978 to 5,416.

The bad autumn and winter of 1916 (known in Germany as the Turnip Winter), which affected European agriculture, but also, most importantly, the poor grain harvest of the same year in the continental Americas, added to Germany's problem with food supplies. Staple foodstuffs such as grain, potatoes, meat and dairy products became so scarce by the winter of 1916 that many people subsisted on a diet of ersatz products that ranged from so-called 'war bread' (*Kriegsbrot*), made from rye and potatoes (and also barley, oats, rice and peameal), to powdered milk. Butter was made from curdled milk, sugar and food colour. Coffee was invented from tree bark, acorns or chicory, tea from raspberry or catnip leaves, textiles from nettles. Cooking oil was concocted from carrots, red beet and turnip; cockchafers and lime wood replaced fats. By the end of the war some eleven thousand ersatz products were on sale in Germany, including thirty-three egg substitutes (the ration for real eggs was one per person per two weeks) and 837 different kinds of 'sausage'.

Captain Leake referred slightingly to these ersatz products in a letter to his mother from his new appointment in HMS *Achilles*: 'Beer and Beef made England and the Empire, so is it likely it can't be maintained without it. Water and sawdust may be all right for dolls. Substitutes have evidently killed the Boche's guts.'

By 1916, 'the German population was surviving on a meagre diet of dark bread, slices of sausage without fat, an individual ration of three pounds of potatoes per week, and turnips'; and in that year the potato crop failed as well.

And it was not just food. Shoes were in particularly short supply. This had a curious side effect in the army, where soldiers would hack off their jackboot heels and post them home to their families: the troops would then draw new boots from army stores. Soap, too, was almost impossible to obtain. Inadequate washing materials meant that many Germans now had to contend with personal lice.

The shortages caused looting and food riots. In Hamburg in March 1916, an observer reported queues of six to eight hundred people outside shops whenever consignments of butter were delivered. The following month there were food riots and fights to obtain scarce goods. Two women were killed and sixteen hospitalised. Protests were not confined to Germany, but also occurred in her Austrian ally's capitals of Vienna and Budapest.

The German government made several attempts to alleviate the worst effects of the blockade. One was the construction of two 'merchant' submarines, designed to carry freight from America to Germany underwater. So optimistic about this new venture were the authorities that they announced that ordinary mail between the USA and the Fatherland could soon be sent by commercial submarine. Named *Bremen* and *Deutschland*, the first-named was sunk without trace, but the second made two successful round trips to the USA before the idea was consigned to history.

The authorities pushed the line that the British blockade was intended to cause starvation, but that by scrimping and avoiding waste this could be prevented. Several hundred public speakers were enrolled to enlighten the *Volk* on the British starvation policy; as a result, Britain quickly became Germany's enemy number one, replacing the Russian Slavic menace which had so preoccupied them in the early days of the fighting. Price controls were introduced as early as October 1914 for bread and cereals, followed swiftly by potatoes, sugar and cattle feed. Price supervisory boards were implemented in September 1915 and by May 1916 a War Food Office was called into being. Lack of co-ordination and lack of food itself brought their efforts to naught. In larger cities, so-called 'war kitchens' provided cheap meals to an impoverished local population. By October 1916 there were 1,437 public kitchens operating across Germany producing nearly two million portions daily.

Another attempt at alleviation of the shortages was the ill thought-out Hindenburg programme, introduced in December 1916, and designed to raise productivity by ordering the compulsory employment of all men between the ages of seventeen and sixty. A complicated system of rationing, which built on the scheme first introduced in the June of the previous year, was aimed at ensuring that some minimum nutritional needs were met. However, the printing of the ration cards proved to be a major undertaking; it required seventy rail cars per annum to haul the 15 tons of paper necessary to print the cards for just the 1.7 million inhabitants of greater Berlin alone. Toy manufacturers proved adept at following the latest trends, at least until raw material shortages stopped them. After food rationing was introduced, German dolls came with a ration-card accessory. The programme also aimed to bring the whole of the population into productive work. Hindenburg himself summed up his goal with the slogan 'He who does not work shall not eat'.

But in reality, the food rationing schemes enjoyed only limited success. The blockade was too tightly enforced. A historian has commented that:

> by autumn of 1916 the machinery of the blockade had reached a high degree of efficiency. The various rationing agreements and agreements with neutral shipping lines were on the whole working well ... As regards food supplies, the winter of 1916–1917 is acknowledged by all to have been in Germany, the worst period of the war.

The German decision to adopt the policy of unrestricted submarine warfare on 1 February 1917, primarily against British trade, has been described as 'the worst decision of the war', although that is contested ground when one considers the disasters of Gallipoli and the Somme, amongst others.

By early 1917 the Allied powers were in anything but a strong position. For France, the butchery of Verdun and the Somme had significantly exhausted their army, and the spring would see riots and strikes within the ranks. For Britain, two years of war, during which she had carried the economically impoverished French, had depleted her gold reserves and other monetary instruments to the point where the Treasury forecast that Britain could be broke by March. And in Russia, the revolutionary fervour was reaching boiling point; little over a month after the unrestricted U-boat campaign commenced, the Tsar would be deposed, and shortly afterwards Russia would seek a peace and withdrawal from the war. Furthermore, the Americans – who had grown even more wealthy supplying all sides with armaments and other materials (its net gain in foreign trade since the start of the war had been

4.5–5.0 billion dollars) – had made it clear that they would regard such unrestricted warfare as the final straw; and the Germans knew that it could force Woodrow Wilson to tip his country into combat on the side of the Entente. But still the U-boat campaign was sanctioned to begin on 1 February. Why?

First, the German command group had been convinced by some clever calculations from Department B-1 (the Economic Warfare Plans group) that within five months Britain could be brought to her knees through lack of food, primarily wheat, as a result of such a campaign. But, just as importantly, the morale of the German nation on the home front was at rock bottom. The Turnip Winter of 1916–1917 had devastated people's faith in their leaders, and the four horsemen of the apocalypse were loose in the land. The leaders of the Imperial Reich, pilloried by public opinion for their inability to prevent or subvent the so-called 'hunger blockade', and seeing the economic and social disorder that it had brought with it, wished ardently to visit this disruption onto Britain for purposes not just of warfare, but of revenge. As one submarine commander put it, the unrestricted undersea war was 'simply to pay off our account against their criminal wish to starve all our people, our women and our children'.

If Britain could be brought to her knees before America's power and money could enter the lists, then the planners believed that Germany could still win the war, or at least secure a profitable and honourable peace. Thus did the Northern Patrol help bring about the decision which did most to force America into the war on the Allied side.

This slow starvation of Germany was used by the Germans as an excuse to the USA for the resumption of unrestricted submarine warfare. The German ambassador to the United States of America, Count von Bernstorff, wrote an exculpatory letter to US Secretary of State Lansing in justification stating that:

> a new situation has thus been created which forces Germany to new decisions. Since two years and a half England is using her naval power for a criminal attempt to force Germany into submission by starvation. In brutal contempt of international law, the group of powers led by England not only curtail the

legitimate trade of their opponents, but they also, by ruthless pressure, compel neutral countries either to altogether forego every trade not agreeable to the Entente Powers, or to limit it according to their arbitrary decrees … the English Government, however, insists upon continuing its war of starvation, which does not at all affect the military power of its opponents, but compels women and children, the sick and the aged, to suffer for their country pains and privations which endanger the vitality of the nation.

It was an admission of weakness which they would much rather not have made.

Commander England of *Orvieto* saw this weakness too: 'This is the culminating point in Prussian militarism – namely that the most brutal warfare is the most humane as it leads to the quickest result,' he confided to his diary. 'Such a measure must be the outcome of desperate need.' He had good reason to hate the German unrestricted submarine campaign, for his father-in-law, Charles Arthur Dingwall, had died in the sinking of *Lusitania* in May 1915.

Some 2,500 calories per day are needed to sustain working life. By 1917 the German rationing schemes offered only a daily diet of 1,100 calories, which was insufficient even for infants. Diseases of malnutrition – scurvy, tuberculosis and dysentery – became commonplace throughout Germany by 1917. In Austria the official ration gave only 850 calories by 1918: 'Too little to live on, too much to die' was the catchphrase.

By the last year of the war, the mortality rate among civilians in Germany was 38 per cent higher than in 1913; tuberculosis was rampant, and, among children, so were rickets and oedema. The collapse of German morale on the Western Front in the autumn of 1918 was in some large measure due to the reports that combatants were receiving about conditions for their families and friends at home, and their shock at seeing the plentiful Allied rations that they captured in their last great offensive of the war (the 1918 *Kaiserschlacht* [Kaiser's battle]).

Britain fared much better, at least until the unrestricted U-boat campaign of 1917. Whilst Germany was suffering from increasingly harsh rationing, the British diet appeared unchanged. The *Daily Telegraph* of 16 January 1915, for instance, published under the headline 'Some Little Luncheons', the following suggested menu: 'Filets de Merlan Frit, Lamb chops a l'Espagnole, Braised Celery and Beef marrow, Parisian Potatoes and Rosaline Soufflé.'

Whilst food shortages did occur from time to time, the government first attempted to control the matter through the encouragement of voluntary restraint. Articles appeared in newspapers during February 1917 indicating that the government's food controller, Lord Devonport, wanted to avoid compulsory rationing, but that there was a need to economise. People were requested to restrict their eating to no more than 4lb of bread or food made from 3lb flour; 2lb 8oz of meat (including bacon and sausages); and 12oz of sugar a week. Fish or eggs, however, were said to be freely available (such quantities would have seemed bounteous to the enemy).

In an early example of 'nudge' social-control techniques, newspapers published recipes for nourishing food that required less meat, like a savoury meat roll made with minced meat, bread and eggs or a stew made with chestnuts. People were encouraged to eat more pulses and to have herrings for breakfast instead of bacon. The rich were asked to set a good example, and hotels and gentlemen's clubs were exhorted to have meatless days.

This is not to suggest that there was no rationing 'pain' in Britain. Under the DORA (Defence of the Realm Act) regulations, it was legislated in April 1917 that the 'manufacture and sale of light pastries, muffins, crumpets, and teacakes is prohibited. Scones must contain no sugar'. No more toasted crumpets for tea then! Furthermore, 'the use of wheat, rice, and rye for other purposes than seed and flour for human consumption is prohibited'. Both of these measures were clearly targeted at preserving flour for the manufacture of bread. Tea shops were also targeted: 'no individual customer shall be served at any meal whatsoever which begins between the hours of 3pm and 6pm with more than 2oz in the whole of bread, cake, bun, scone, and biscuit'.

There were long queues for certain foodstuffs on occasion but when a system of rationing was introduced, first in London at the beginning of 1918 and then in the remainder of the country later in the year, it worked within reason. Administered by area food control committees, rationing encompassed such commodities as margarine and butter (4oz per head per week) and tea (only 1½oz per head per week). At no time was Britain ever to face the starvation that afflicted Germany and her allies, although it was a close-run thing in early 1917, and it was only the belated adoption of convoy tactics in May, in the face of the German unrestricted submarine campaign, that prevented such an eventuality. The UK only issued meat ration cards in February 1918 and bread, even at the height of the German U-boat campaign, was never rationed.

German consumer price inflation over the period 1914–1919 had reached 300 per cent, compared to just over 100 per cent in Britain. German exports over the same period had fallen to zero (Britain's had increased by 180 per cent), and her industrial production was down by nearly 70 per cent. Blockade had destroyed Germany's will and capacity to resist. And the resultant food shortages destroyed the health of her population, paving the way for the influenza epidemic of 1918 that was to kill 400,000 German civilians.

PART THREE
A Desperate Battle

The ultimate objects of British Naval Policy are defined as:

Firstly to bring pressure to bear on the enemy people so as to compel their government to come to terms and secondly to resist the pressure applied by them so that we may carry on the war undisturbed. In order to achieve these objects British naval power must be directed into the following channels.

The protection of the Sea Communications of the Allied armies more particularly in France where the main offensive lies.

Prevention of enemy trade as a means of handicapping his military operation and exerting pressure on the mass of his people.

Protection of British and Allied trade on which depends the supply of munitions and food to the allied armies and people Resistance to Invasion and Raids.

Operations Division, Naval Staff, 'Present Naval Policy', 17 September 1917, quoted in Arthur Marder, *From the Dreadnought to Scapa Flow*, volume V.

Yarrowdale and Prisoners, 1916–1917

Whilst the Royal Navy was helping to inflict the Turnip Winter – the worst in living memory – on Germany, Dohna-Schlodien continued his one-man war against British trade. He had captured SS *Yarrowdale* on 11 December 1916 and sent her back to Germany loaded with prisoners from his prizes. He had seen in her many similarities to his beloved *Moewe* – size, speed, accommodation, 'ordinariness'.

She was a 4,625grt vessel, capable of 13 knots, built in Newcastle in 1912 for the Glasgow firm of Mackill, Roberts and Co. When she was taken she was fully loaded with 117 motor vehicles, 30,000 rolls of barbed wire, 3,300 tons of steel bars and 6,300 cases of rifle cartridges, a cargo of great value to the Allied – and now the German – war effort. Dohna-Schlodien loaded 469 prisoners on board her (it took all day in violent seas on 13 December), including eighty-nine American citizens, and despatched her and her cargo to Swinemünde the next day.

Yarrowdale's voyage to Germany was not without incident. The ship was compelled by a bad storm to anchor in Swedish waters and a Swedish officer came on board to demand that they leave; the ship's captain, Acting Leutnant Badewitz, protested that they were just a coaling vessel and as such were entitled to be there. The Swede 'walked up and down the deck with the captain, who was smoking a pipe … while this officer was on board the Germans stood with their revolvers levelled at the prisoners in the hold'. The Swedish officer found nothing untoward and left the vessel unmolested. Badewitz had already shown his abilities when commanding the prize *Westburn* in February, which was used to ferry prisoners to Tenerife during *Moewe*'s first cruise. After releasing his captives, he destroyed the ship to prevent it falling into British hands, was interned by the Spanish authorities, managed to escape and rejoined *Moewe*.

The passage of *Yarrowdale* through the Northern Blockade was another event in which shipyard industrial action was seen to play a part. Tupper was to explain that on 24–25 December, when he assumed she had passed by, he had only six of twenty-three vessels under his command available, in part due to delays in refitting owing to, unbelievably, a strike by boilermakers at Liverpool.

On arrival in port, the prisoners were detained on the ship, but on 5 January 1917 they were transported south. 'For food they were only given soup, which was bad and uneatable, a few slices of potato bread and water'; in this, as noted in Chapter 14, they were probably on a par with their hosts. They were quartered in a large barracks surrounded by barbed wire. It was bitterly cold and the mattresses they were given were so wet and dirty that many men preferred to sleep on the floor. 'The next morning the men were benumbed with cold and famished by hunger.'

The majority of the American prisoners were sailors or horse-handlers. But four were professional men – two doctors, John Davis from Columbus, Missouri and H D Snyder from Norfolk, Virginia – and two vets, Orville McKim of Watertown, New York, and Richard Zabrinski. As physicians and vets they were considered by the structured Teutonic mind to be deserving of separate treatment and were ranked as officers. As such they were confined in a different camp to their compatriots, in the centre of Karlsruhe, where apparently they were at risk from Allied aerial bombardments aimed at the town's two railway stations.

The detention of both sets of Americans had now become a major diplomatic row. America was still neutral at this time and under prize law her citizens should not be detained as prisoners of war. But the Germans insisted that, as they had been captured on board defensively armed merchantmen, and as they treated such vessels as warships, then the Americans rights as neutrals were forfeit. The American State Department, however, 'held throughout that a vessel cannot be classed as a warship unless it is under naval orders and the naval flag and is manned by naval crews'.

There now ensued a torrent of telegrams and diplomatic notes between Secretary of State Robert Lansing in Washington, the US ambassador in Berlin, James W Gerard, and the German Foreign Office. Gerard wrote to the Berlin government four times between 20 and 26 January without eliciting a reply. Eventually, an evasive response effectively said that they didn't have the crew lists and the Imperial Navy weren't in any hurry to supply them. But the Germans were still hopeful of keeping America out of the war and some pretext needed to be found to get them off this particular hook. On 4 February Gerard was able to telegraph that 'he had just been informed by Count Montgelas of the Foreign Office that the American prisoners taken on *Yarrowdale* would be at once released for the reason that they could not have known at the date of sailing that it was the intention of Germany to regard and treat armed merchantmen as warships'. Honour was apparently satisfied. It was not, however, the end of the matter.

On 12 February the Swiss legation in Washington, acting for the German government, transmitted this message to Lansing: 'The immediate release of about 70 Americans, brought in as prisoners of war by the steamer *Yarrowdale* is conditional to the German vessels in American waters not being seized and their crews not being interned.' Ambassador Willard in Madrid now got in on the act. On 17 February he sent a message to Washington to the effect that he had been told that the prisoners would be released imminently.

Lansing, before the war a lawyer and a vigorous advocate in favour of the principles of freedom of the seas and the rights of neutral nations, blew his diplomatic top. His reply escalated the stakes for Germany:

Ambassador Willard is directed to transmit the following to the Spanish Ambassador at Berlin through the Spanish Foreign Office. If *Yarrowdale* prisoners have not been released please make a formal demand in the name of the United States for their immediate release. If they are not promptly released and allowed to cross the frontier without further delay, please state to the Foreign Minister that this policy of the Imperial Government, if continued apparently without the slightest justification, will oblige the Government of the United States to consider what measures it may be necessary to take in order to obtain satisfaction for the continued detention of these innocent American citizens.

The Germans replied that the prisoners had been released on 16 February, but that one of them contracted typhus and therefore all were detained in quarantine in Brandenberg. They would be released when the quarantine period was over. And so eventually they were, leaving Germany via Sweden on 8 March. War was now imminent and perhaps this was reflected in the tone of the telegrams now being sent. From the American legation in Berne, Minister Stovall reported on 16 March that:

> no complaint was made by the men of *Yarrowdale* of their treatment while on the high seas or in camp near Swindemunde, which was their first camp. They were first transferred to Brandenburg about January 10, where, according to their statement, their treatment by the officers was very harsh. It was impossible for them to keep warm. They were kept standing in the cold and snow. Their food consisted, after one cup of coffee in the morning, mostly of boiled, frosted cabbage; once a week beans; and once a week mush.

They denied the presence of any infectious disease.

The four Americans held in Karlsruhe had travelled separately and were not detained by problems of quarantine. They arrived in Copenhagen on 3 March and were placed under the care of the British consul. On arrival they were 'practically destitute and had only the clothes they stood up in ... They lived for more than two months in prison camp in Germany on the meagre prison fare provided by the German government without food parcels which lighted the condition of existence of other prisoners of war'.

Minister Stovall continued his reportage on 18 March, writing that 'the most cruel and heartless treatment was accorded the shipwrecked American sailors from the moment of their arrival in Germany January 3rd'. Three weeks later, the two countries were at war.

Meanwhile, work had proceeded apace on *Yarrowdale*. She was given a heavy armament rig, false doors and shutters were fitted to hide her weapons, radio equipment fitted, provisions and ammunition taken on board. On 9 January 1917 she was commissioned as the auxiliary cruiser *Leopard* and given the disguised identity of the Norwegian ship *Rena*. This was a peculiar choice of alias, as it had been used before by *Greif* (*vide supra*). The real *Rena* was then off the coast of South Africa, having arrived at Port Natal sometime around 28 February.

And on 7 March, three days before *Moewe* was to fight its defining desperate battle with *Otaki*, *Leopard* crept slowly from her lair.

Of Ships and Men, 1917

The 2nd Cruiser Squadron had been detailed to assist the 10th Cruiser Squadron in the Northern Patrol and blockade at the end of October 1916; Jellicoe, perhaps realising that the ships could not fight with the Grand Fleet as Jutland had demonstrated, told off the squadron for duties based at Swarbacks Minn. Their tasking orders stated that 'the objective of the Northern Patrol was to intercept enemy raiders and submarine supply ships attempting to break out into the Atlantic AND to send in vessels with cargoes of enemy origin or destination'.

It was not a duty that brought much comfort to the sailors, as the weather conditions made life on the big ships as uncomfortable as it had for the old *Edgar*s in 1914. On 3 November 1916 one of them reported that '*Achilles* rolled 30 degrees to 25 degrees and frequently put her broadsides turrets under water. Mess decks were awash and water got down through the downdraughts to the ventilating fans in the ammunition passage.'* But they stuck it out, patrolling in three sections, each of one cruiser, and come March they were still about their tasking.

The Admiralty had a certain amount of information as to both *Moewe*'s attempted return and the concurrent planned breakout of *Leopard*. This was gleaned through Room 40, the secret naval intelligence-gathering and decrypting department run by Captain

*Even battleships were not immune from the weather in the northern regions. In the summer of 1915, the 15,000 ton pre-dreadnought battleship *Albemarle*, out of Scapa and heading for the Dardanelles, was hit by seas in the Pentland Firth which swept away half her bridge, together with several officers and men, including her commander. She had to be towed back to Scapa Flow.

Reginald 'Blinker' Hall, a man of whom it could truly be said that he did as much as anyone to ensure America's entry into the war, as well as providing priceless intelligence of German intentions, based on their somewhat intemperate use of radio. Indeed, there had been an alert on 24 January 1917 when Commander England recorded 'big spread for a raider, we are northernmost ship'.

Another warning came in March and as a result, Admiral David Beatty, now commander-in-chief at Scapa following Jellicoe's sublimation to the post of First Sea Lord, was ordered to strengthen the Northern Patrol and to keep a watch on the Norwegian coast. Beatty at once sent two cruisers to patrol to the north of the Shetlands along the meridian of 1° W, and detached the 4th Light Cruiser Squadron with four destroyers to watch the Norwegian coast between the Nord Fjord and the Sogne Fjord.

This proved a fruitless task, for both groups returned on 14 March having sighted nothing, and were not ordered to renew the patrol. Meanwhile, on 11 March, Rear Admiral Sydney Fremantle (known throughout the Navy as 'my boy Syd' since his father, also an admiral, had once so referred to him), now in command of the 2nd Cruiser Squadron, sent a new deployment order to three of his charges. From receipt of order, and until relief arrived, the patrol line north of the Shetlands, which had become the 2nd Cruiser Squadron's regular duty, was to be occupied by *Achilles*, *Minotaur* and *Duke of Edinburgh*. The ships sailed from Swarbacks Minn and took up their patrol stations, each cruiser being accompanied by a small armed boarding steamer. The time passed uneventfully in the heaving seas, cold and grey skies. At the far northern end of the patrol line was *Achilles* and her consort, *Dundee*. Both ships had been busy, as during 12–15 March they had intercepted and boarded steamers. The strain of the duty showed in the fact that *Achilles* had nineteen men on the sick list. Now it was 16 March, one day before their planned relief, an event no doubt looked forward to with anticipation by the two ships' crews.

The *Dundee*

The advent of the 2nd Cruiser Squadron, with their large armoured cruisers, also necessitated the introduction of a new type of vessel to act alongside them, the Armed Boarding Steamer (ABS).

Armoured cruisers were big and heavy ships, unsuited to the delicate manoeuvring and boat management that was required to stop and search interdicted merchant ships. Additionally, when approaching to perform the 'visit and search' and stopping to lower a boat, they laid themselves open to a devastating surprise attack which could render useless or sink an expensive piece of naval hardware. And so they were partnered with small and agile vessels, better able to close and detain a suspect cargo ship. They were civilian craft, often former Scottish small coastal cargo and passenger vessels (although one, *Amsterdam*, was an ex-Channel packet and bounced like a cork in the heavy seas), pressed into service for the duration, not given 'HMS' prefixes and crewed entirely by RNR or, more commonly, RNVR men. Such was SS *Dundee*. She had been built by Caledon shipbuilders at their Dundee yards and was launched on 24 August 1911. In November of that year she had entered service with the Dundee, Perth & London Shipping Company as a small cargo/passenger carrier and sailed for them until the outbreak of the war. Of 2,187grt and capable of 15 knots, fast enough to catch most merchant ships, she would encounter, she was lightly armed with two 4in naval guns and two 3pdrs, and was, of course, completely unarmoured.

She was captained by 44-year-old Commander Selwyn M Day RNR, a London-born merchant mariner of long experience. Day was a time-served seaman and RNR officer. He had held a number of merchant commands and had belonged to the reserve since 1891, when he signed up aged eighteen. Day had briefly come to public notice in 1906 when he was the mate on SS *Ecuador* out of Liverpool, which stranded at the port of Ballenita, occasioning a British Board of Trade inquiry which exonerated the captain and his mates, including young Selwyn. He had held the rank of commander RNR since 31 December 1916 and his appointment to *Dundee* followed four days later.

Dundee's crew was short of two officers and eleven men for some reason; one of the missing officers was Day's second in command and his place had been taken by an Australian RNVR member, 27-year-old Sub Lieutenant (Acting Lieutenant) Frederick Herman Lawson. Lawson, who had been born in Birkenhead, near Adelaide, South Australia, and a resident of Largs Bay in the same

146

state, had travelled halfway around the world to get involved in the war on the British side, despite given names which suggested some Germanic heritage. One of five children, with a widowed mother, he had left Adelaide as third officer on SS *Twickenham* and, after the outbreak of war, had served on transport duties before he joined the reserve in August 1915. He was subsequently gazetted with the rank of sub lieutenant RNR on 24 August 1915. Lawson had been continuously involved since then, serving on *King Orry*, another armed boarding steamer, and an ex-Isle of Man steam packet, based at Swarbacks Minn, until transferring to *Dundee* on 2 February 1917. His previous skipper had obviously thought well of him, for he had been recommended for promotion to acting lieutenant at the end of August of the previous year.

HMS *Achilles*

Achilles had yet to fire a shot in anger. During the battle of Jutland, she had been in dock undergoing a refit and thus missed the action. This may have been a blessing in disguise, for three of her sisters were sunk that day with the loss of 2,493 men.

She was a *Warrior*-class vessel, launched in 1905, armed with six 9.2in guns and four 7.5in, together with three torpedo tubes. She was considered a good sea boat and a steady gun platform and had a design speed of 23 knots.

As a type, the armoured cruisers were obsolescent, if not obsolete. Jutland had proved them highly vulnerable when in a fleet engagement. They were a class of warship developed in the late nineteenth century, designed like other types of cruisers to operate as a long-range, independent unit, capable of defeating any ship apart from a battleship, and fast enough to outrun any battleships it encountered. Armoured cruisers were distinguished from other types of cruiser by their belt armour of iron (or later steel) plating on much of the hull to protect the ship from shellfire, much like the protection method of battleships, and differed from the latter class by their designed long range, speed and coal-carrying capability. Such large, armoured cruisers were made obsolete by the development of the battlecruiser, fast, heavily armed capital ships, and the increasing speeds of battleships themselves, as turbine and (eventually) oil technology became prevalent. It was perhaps this fact which made Jellicoe and Beatty happy to send them from the Grand Fleet and relegate them to the quotidian duties of the Northern Patrol. But nonetheless, the armament carried by *Achilles* would be formidable against any smaller craft.

Her captain was Francis Martin-Leake, the commander of the unfortunate *Pathfinder*, encountered in Chapter 6, who had been somewhat fortuitous in escaping that disaster with his life. He had spent a period of convalescence on the hospital yacht *Sheelah*, which was owned by Admiral David Beatty's wife Ethel, before being posted to Portland, training up M-class destroyers. On 19 February 1915 he took command of *Achilles*, replacing Captain A L Cay, who was to die the following year when *Invincible* blew up at Jutland.

He was a descendant of one of Queen Anne's admirals, Sir John Leake (who fought in the War of the Spanish Succession and became First Lord of the Admiralty in 1710), and the son of a successful barrister and JP, Stephen Martin-Leake, who owned both Thorpe Hall in Essex (sold to Julian Byng, later Field Marshal and First Viscount Byng of Vimy, in 1913) and Marshalls in Standon, Hertfordshire. His brother Arthur had become one of only three men in history to win the Victoria Cross twice – in 1902 during the Boer War and in 1914 at Ypres, during service with the Royal Army Medical Corps.

Francis was a small man, highly popular amongst his men. After completing the war course at the Royal Naval College in 1912, he was assessed as fourth out of eight captains in the order of merit, and summarised as 'thoughtful, very attentive and capable'. A fellow officer described him thus: 'quiet, unassuming, and reserved, he combined firmness and great ability with a tendency to mercy for those who were less able to help themselves in a way that made him a real leader of men'.

He was certainly a man who was prepared to take a stand on his opinions, even if it meant annoying First Lord of the Admiralty Winston Churchill. Whilst in command of *Pathfinder*, Leake was ordered to Irish waters at the time of the Curragh incident (a proto-mutiny of the officers of the Dublin garrison) in March 1914 and, in common with many other officers and men at this time of unrest over the Irish Home Rule bill, felt bound to state that in the event of hostilities with the Ulster Volunteers (the Unionists, who were against Ireland being granted home rule), he would be unable to participate in subsequent operations. News of his message quickly leaked to the press, much to the annoyance of Churchill at the Admiralty, who sent him a blistering note of chastisement. It did not, however, effect Leake's determination.

SMS *Leopard*

Leopard had been given an even heavier armament outfit than *Moewe*. She mounted no fewer than five 15cm guns forward and four 8.8cm guns, with four side-launched torpedo tubes and space for mines. All of her weapons were concealed by false hatches, deckhouses, etc, and her armament (roughly equivalent to five 6in and four 4in British naval guns) gave her a considerable weight of fire when matched against anything she was likely to encounter less than a first-class cruiser. She was, of course, unarmoured, but had been fitted with seven watertight compartments which, if she was damaged, would give her better powers of flotation than *Moewe*.

Her captain was an unusually tall 38-year-old Saxon, Korvetten-Kapitan Hans von Laffert, a colleague and good friend of Dohna-Schlodien. A married man with a daughter aged five, another member of the minor German aristocracy, he took with him as his second in command Leutnant Reinhold Badewitz, who had sailed *Yarrowdale* and her prisoners back to Germany, another fourteen officers and a crew of 304 men. His orders required him to operate against British trade off the coast of the River Plate estuary and the Cape of Good Hope and when no longer able to fulfil his role, to sail for Argentina, Brazil or Chile for internment, recognising that a return to Germany would be nigh on impossible.

The German naval staff had given von Laffert intelligence about the increase in British patrolling in northern waters and left the decision to sail to him. Immediately before his departure he signalled, 'have taken into consideration in all respects augmented enemy patrols. Take the responsibility nevertheless for the success of the enterprise'.

*   *   *

These then were the ships and men whom fate was to bring together in the Norwegian Sea, two hundred miles northeast of the Faroe Islands. A heavily armed raider, a small steamer and a large – if outdated – cruiser, slowly converging on a patch of wind-wracked sea; one trying to sneak out, two trying to catch her.

17

First Contact, March 1917

It was grey. The sky was grey, the sea was grey, the light seemed grey. An occasional snow squall provided little variation. The temperature was a little above freezing at 38°F (3.3°C). The wind was from the southeast, force 4 to 5, the seas moderate, some grey spray from the wave crests splashing the side of *Achilles*. She was making 10 knots, her consort *Dundee* within visibility range to the south. All through the night and morning they had patrolled their line, heading south from midnight to 0600 and now north, making a slight zigzag as they went along to throw off any potential underwater attacker. It was 1145; in fifteen minutes they would reverse course and start patrolling to the south again. Six hours south, six hours north; and then the same again, a grey, dull patrol in a grey seascape. It was cold and boring; but tomorrow they could go home.

Chief Petty Officer Isted was on watch duty. He had been in the navy since boyhood; boredom, he knew, was part of the job. But that didn't mean that either he or his fellow watchkeepers could ever relax. So it was no surprise that he was the first to see a ship, nine miles off, at the limit of visibility. She was stern on, heading north. He sang out the sighting report.

Captain Leake ordered *Achilles* around and signalled to *Dundee* to close to the cruiser. He increased his speed to 15 knots, but made little impact on the distance to the stranger. That in itself was puzzling; he had not come across that many ordinary cargo vessels of such speed in those waters. Leake ordered revolutions for 18 knots and in the engine room the stokers began to bend their backs.

By 1345 he had to make a change of direction to keep out of the rough water caused by the stranger's wake and at 1400 Leake ordered her to heave to, which she did. Further instructions told her to steer west by south, and at 1435 she was again told to stop. Leake manoeuvred his big cruiser to some three miles distant and ordered *Dundee* to investigate.

On board the little steamer, Commander Day considered the intercepted vessel. She was painted black, with some white on the upper works, and had a large funnel, black with two thin white bands. There were eight lifeboats amidships and two aft, two masts with cross trees and long cargo derricks. She was flying the Norwegian flag and had the words RENA NORGE painted on both sides of her hull. He thought that she looked large for these waters. On checking Lloyd's register, he found that there was a *Rena* but that the vessel in front of him seemed larger than Lloyd's stated 3,000 tons. Furthermore she had no wireless visible, no superfluous woodwork and had steamed steadily at 13 knots for several hours, unusual for a cargo vessel. On board *Achilles*, they noted that her paintwork looked new.

Day continued his scrutiny, something nagging at the back of his mind. Then it came to him. He thought that she resembled a photograph of *Moewe* taken by a crew member of *Dramatist*, sunk on 18 December the previous year, which he had seen in the *Daily Mail* on 3 March. A marine gunner, Lance Corporal Short, noticed and reported that the letters 'N' on the stranger's sides were inverted, as if they had been painted on at sea. It was all very odd, but hardly the basis for opening fire.

By now *Dundee* was about two miles from the stranger and Day began to prepare to launch his boarding boat. Normally, the task of leading the boarding and search party would have fallen to his (absent) second in command. Acting Lieutenant Lawson had no hesitation in volunteering for the job, as the officer on whom the task would otherwise devolve was very inexperienced. The boarding party assembled, Lawson and a crew of five seamen to row over to *Rena*.

Dundee was a Shetland-based vessel and Shetland RNR men formed a proportion of her crew. They were much prized for their skill with small boats and thus four of the five-man crew of the boarding whaler were Shetlanders, all called Anderson (in all there were six Andersons in *Dundee*'s crew). Two were unrelated, Henry and Robert John; Henry's brother, another Robert, was also from *Dundee*. Two were fourth cousins, Henry James and Magnus John (see Appendix 5). All were rated seaman. The other member of the boat's crew was a Liverpudlian, RNVR Able Seaman Alfred Birchall.

The six men took their places in the whaler and Day towed it to within half a mile of *Rena*, releasing it on her port quarter and maintaining *Dundee*'s position such that his ship was at right angles to the stern of the Norwegian ship. In this way, he would if necessary be able to fire a full broadside whilst presenting the smallest possible target for any aggressive action by his quarry. He had all his gun crews closed up and ready. Because of the depleted number of officers on board, there were no officers of quarters available to take command of *Dundee*'s guns. That task devolved to the gunlayers themselves, one RFR, one RNVR and two RNR. Another Anderson, John George, second cousin to Henry Anderson of the boarding party, was among them.

Dundee cast off her boat at 1442 and simultaneously commenced a signal dialogue with *Rena*. At 1450 she sent, 'Pay attention to signals'. This was ignored and so a blank round was fired. 1459, 'What is your cargo'; 'General' was the response. 1510, 'Where are you from'; 'Mobile'. 1530, 'When did you leave'; no response. Also at 1530 Leake sent to Day, 'Have you sent boat?' which received an affirmative reply, no doubt rather acerbically.

Commander Day was now a worried man. *Rena*'s responses were evasive at best. And now he had lost sight of his sea boat and its boarding crew, which had made its way round to the starboard and lee side and was now out of view. Additionally, Day had to keep adjusting his position for the other vessel was:

> trying to defeat my object of maintaining a position (for attack) close up to the weather quarter and heading across his stern, and he constantly moved the propellers, slewing to port or starboard. Keeping station thus we awaited some sign from the boarding officer or the boat, which was, of course, on the lee side, and could not be seen by us.

Commander Day ordered his signalman to keep a close watch on *Rena*'s rudder and screws for any sign of a sudden attempt to swing to port.

On board *Rena*, von Laffert stood with two other officers on the open bridge. He had not wanted to stop, but against the big armoured cruiser he was effectively helpless, its weaponry, 6in of side armour, and superior speed making it an adversary that he could not hope to defeat without some act of stupidity on the cruiser's part. He watched as the boarding party came round to his starboard side and the accommodation ladder. Any thorough search would quickly expose the myth of his alleged pacific Norwegian purpose. He only had two choices, surrender or fight. And German officers do not, as Captain Reymann of the *Kaiser Wilhelm der Grosse* had said to Buller of the *Highflyer*, surrender.

1 8

Battle, March 1917

At 1540 a signalman on board *Dundee* yelled out, 'She's moving sir'. A roil of froth at the stern of *Rena* showed her screws revolving strongly and she slewed to port. At the same time, Day heard a sharp slapping noise as the flag boards on *Rena*'s sides fell outwards on their hinges and banged against the hull, revealing the weapons within and thus becoming *Leopard* once more. Of his boat's crew he could see no sign.

'Open fire!' yelled Day, and then, 'Half speed ahead'. The response from his gunners was instant. Closed up and ready for over an hour they had the range and distance off pat. The old 4in weapons roared out and the very first shot from the aft gun hit *Leopard*'s portside battery, causing an explosion and gout of smoke. The forward gun hit the engine room producing a rush of steam. The 3pdrs joined in, aiming for the bridge and upper works.

'Torpedo!' shouted an agonised watchkeeper; von Laffert had fired two from his port launchers. Their aim was good, but Day's sudden call for speed had upset the firing calculations. One torpedo passed 20ft astern of *Dundee*, the other missed by 50ft.

On *Achilles*, Leake desperately manoeuvred to get into a firing position. She had been 5,300yds away from *Leopard*'s starboard side heading south when Leake heard the firing. He swung her round onto a westerly course and opened fire at 1547 with his full port broadside, four 9.2in and two 7.5in. After finding the range he switched from common shell to trotyl HE for his big guns and lyddite HE for the 7.5in guns, firing three salvoes a minute. *Achilles*'s torpedo department joined in at 1555, firing an

18in mark VII which appeared to hit forward of the *Leopard*'s bridge works.

The German vessel was taking a terrible punishment. She disappeared behind a pall of smoke, the pinprick flames of her own broadside glowing dimly within the shroud. She nonetheless managed to launch a third torpedo, this time at *Achilles*, which was by now near her top speed of 20 knots and which porpoised off her port quarter. *Achilles*' lookouts reported a submarine periscope (periscopitis was an epidemic disease in the Royal Navy) and a capsized boat. At 1600, unable to see what was happening through the pall of fire and smoke, Leake ordered a check-fire and noted in the log that *Leopard/Rena* was heavily on fire.

Dundee, meanwhile, had fired forty-four 4in and twenty-five 3pdr shells at about 1,000yds range without reply. But now she found herself crossing what Day thought was the raider's stern, only to find that she had turned through 180 degrees and was broadside on to him. What was more, *Dundee* was now in *Achilles*' line of fire. *Leopard* fired three broadsides at *Dundee* and launched another torpedo, but she was burning from stem to stern and none of them hit the little steamer, which was now downwind and wreathed in protective smoke. Day hastily turned away to the west, his after 4in continuing to fire at the enemy.

On board *Leopard* it was chaos. Fires were burning everywhere, power had largely been lost to the hydraulic systems, dead and dying littered the decks. Five petty officers huddled under the bridge works on the disengaged side. One quickly wrote a note and all of them signed it. They pushed the paper into a glass bottle, sealed it, and threw it over the side of the ship and into the cold, deep waters.

Achilles resumed fire at 1611, recording many more hits, but *Leopard*, although on fire from end to end by now, refused to die. Gun flashes of two different calibres remained visible. The Norwegian ensign continued to fly. At 1618, with *Leopard* completely hidden from view by flame and smoke, Leake ordered another ceasefire.

As the *Official History* noted:

the raider was now a doomed vessel. She was often hidden from view in clouds of black smoke, and several times the gunners in the *Achilles* had to check their fire. For nearly an hour the Germans stood up against the stream of shell which poured into their ship; her internal fires, and the bursts of the heavy shell from the *Achilles*, started explosions and sent up jets of flame through the smoke clouds which rose out of her.

After her turn to the west, *Dundee* fell in astern of *Achilles* and fired off the remainder of her ammunition, checking at 1615. Leake then ordered her out of the way, once more to westward. At 1625 Day reported by short-range radio that he too had seen a submarine. Worried that he needed to finish the job or be a target of a German submarine attack himself, Leake resumed firing. *Leopard* was blazing furiously, oil was pouring out of her and setting the sea ablaze, she was glowing red-hot forward: 'when she began to settle down it seemed to some that the whole of her fore-part was red-hot; others thought that it was melting'.

At 1633 she suddenly rolled to port and sank, more or less horizontally and in a fiery inferno. The watchkeepers noticed that her bottom was very clean. As Day noted in his report, 'the raider was a mass of flame, and obviously a doomed ship, although she continued to fight with apparently but one gun'. *Leopard* had gone down fighting.

She had absorbed a terrible punishment. Apart from the smaller calibre weapons of *Dundee*, *Achilles* had fired 192 rounds of heavy shell at her, rounds designed to sink armoured naval vessels. She had taken a torpedo hit too.

There were no casualties on board either British ship. But Day was still concerned for his boat's crew. At 1615 he had first asked Leake if he could close and pick up his boat. *Achilles* replied, 'Look out for mines', but then resumed firing, rendering such activity void. At 1647 Day again requested permission to look for his boat and receiving no reply repeated his request at 1655. As both ships vacated the area, Leake refused, stating, 'I regret that we were close to the raider and steamed around her and could see nothing of your boats; saw two floating mines and as submarine was seen, search is not justifiable.' Twelve minutes later, at 1714, Day asked that destroyers be ordered up to search for his missing men ('Submit destroyers be sent to look for our boat'). This time Leake didn't even reply.

There can be little doubt that *Dundee* fought bravely. But if she had been on her own, although she might have damaged *Leopard* enough to cause her to return to port, the British ship would have undoubtedly been sunk. She had already fired off all her 4in ammunition during the encounter. The hulking presence of the big cruiser had made it a battle that von Laffert could never have won. His only choices were die or surrender. He chose, and chose for his crew too, to die. As the official historian noted, 'the Germans fought on without any sign of surrender. They could certainly have yielded without dishonour before the end came'.

There were no survivors from von Laffert's ship. Nor were there any from the boarding party. The possible presence of a submarine weighed against any search for men in the water. Day reported:

> With the utmost regret I have to report that Lieut Lawson, RNR, and the boat's crew who volunteered to accept the extreme risk entailed by a boarding operation under such conditions, are missing, having undoubtedly been forced into the raider and lost with her. The boat was observed empty at the commencement of the action as we followed round the stern of the enemy.

A later writer commented:

> Lieutenant Lawson and his crew perished with the Germans: he was doubtless made a prisoner when he went alongside the raider. He knew what he was doing when he volunteered to board so suspicious a ship, and he would never have wished his friends to hold their hands for his sake. He and his men must have spent their last moments of life in full knowledge of the success which they had bought.

Was that really a comfort?

And shortly afterwards, Mrs Mary Jane Lawson of Largs Bay, Adelaide, Frederick Lawson's widowed mother, received a dreadful telegram.

Pro patria mori?

Aftermath

There is no way of knowing what happened on board *Leopard* as battle was joined. At the commencement of the action, von Laffert was on the bridge with two other officers. These would probably be his navigating and gunnery officers. *Dundee*'s first salvo exploded in his port gun battery and the 3pdrs fired immediately at the raider's bridge. It is possible that this caused injury to von Laffert and his key officers at the very start of the action and disrupted *Leopard*'s command and control system. Certainly, it is true that *Leopard* made no reply to *Dundee*'s gunfire (after firing her initial two torpedoes) until forty-four 4in and twenty-five 3pdr shells had been expended by the British ship. The BL 4in Mk VII gun fired a 31lb lyddite explosive shell. The 3-pdr Hotchkiss gun fired a shell, as the name indicates, one tenth of the weight of the 4in (3.1lbs) but at a maximum rate of thirty per minute. At 1,000yds range a goodly proportion of both calibres *must* have hit *Leopard* and she would be severely impacted.

Proof for the disruption of fighting abilities would seem to lie in the fact that von Laffert never managed to salvo fire his guns until some twenty minutes after battle was joined and only then three salvoes (one over, two short) from the port side battery of three or four guns. By which time, of course, he was also being drenched in heavy gunfire from *Achilles*.

Given the weight of gunfire aimed at the bridge, it seems safe to assume that central command was knocked out fairly early in the engagement and that individual gun captains or quarters officers eventually fought *Leopard*'s battle. And much power and propulsion were probably lost soon after *Dundee* started firing. Her after 4in had concentrated throughout the battle on the site of the engine room, which had also been hit by the fore gun at the start of the shooting. By Leake's first check-fire at 1600, the raider must already have been a charnel house and with little or no power to move guns, or to provide electricity or firefighting capacity.

Leopard fought under the Norwegian flag she was flying as part of her disguise. Neither British ship noted any attempt to raise the Imperial German Naval ensign, which von Laffert would surely have wished to have done. Nor did the German ship make any attempt at surrender, despite the comment (*vide supra*) in the

Official History that they could 'have yielded without dishonour', and the opportunity to do so provided by *Achilles*' check-fire at 1600. Again, this seems to point to a loss or disruption of command. Conceivably, the commanding officers were by this point dead or incapacitated.

Likewise, there is no knowledge of what happened to Lieutenant Lawson and his boarding crew. It is likely that as they came round the lee side and boarded, they were overwhelmed by a superior force of armed men and locked below under guard. As *Leopard* quickly turned into a butcher's shop and fire spread throughout the ship, it is inconceivable that they did not make some attempt to escape; whether they perished in that attempt or in the fiery furnace that had once been a German raider will never be known. They may even have been killed or injured by their own ship's shellfire. No other boarding party was lost in such a fashion. They were the unlucky ones.

As noted above, no search for survivors had been conducted because of the assumed presence of a submarine (although Beatty was later to dismiss this sighting report stating that it was probably an oil cask). But between 1845 and 1910 *Achilles* had picked up a repeated broadcast on the 400m wavelength, strength 10: '5K5K5K – 1996 – 9K – IMIK.' It was most probably a German submarine close by, looking for the raider it was to rendezvous with and give assistance to.

Day had sailed shorthanded and was now down another officer and five men. One result was that he no longer knew where he was. At 1734 he signalled Leake, 'Please give me position; we have two officers only on board and are eleven short of deck ratings'. Leake replied, offering to lend him an officer and eight men. Still smarting from being forbidden from looking for his lost sheep, Commander Day declined. It is possible that feelings against Captain Leake in particular, and *Achilles* in general, were running high at that point. Nonetheless, Leake signalled Commander Day the following morning: 'Many thanks for your assistance yesterday and fully appreciate the difficult position from which you extracted *Dundee* yesterday'.

Leake also reported the success by radio to Scapa. Beatty signalled congratulations; the Admiralty, and in particular Room 40, were desperate, however, to know the raider's real identity. Had they got *Moewe* returning, or a new raider venturing out? Nobody knew. Likewise, the Germans were unaware that they had lost their latest raider. After interviewing both of his commanding officers, Beatty erroneously concluded that the ship had been incoming. He also surmised that there had been no submarine so close to the North Pole. *Moewe* and Dohna-Schlodien had, in fact, passed quite close to the position of *Leopard*'s sinking on 17–18 March on their way home, perhaps benefitting from a more relaxed attitude by the Northern Patrol after they had made their kill.

Give that the site of the sinking was only 108 miles from the Arctic Circle, no one held out any hope that survivors would have made their way to safety. But the dead did not disappear without any trace. On 5 June the 'message in a bottle' signed by the five petty officers of *Leopard* was washed ashore near Tromsø. It was sent to Germany where, on 13 June, the signatures were authenticated by relatives. The text read: 'In action with British cruiser. Fighting for the glory and honour of Germany. A last greeting to our relatives'. At this point the Imperial Navy realised that *Leopard* was most probably lost and issued 'next of kin' letters.

And *Dundee* finally found some trace of her missing crewmen. On 8 June she intercepted the Norwegian ship *Solborg*, which had picked up a boat two days beforehand. The boarding party recognised it, and it was offered to them and returned to the ship. The only remains of the six crewmen were a cutlass frog, a broken lamp and one rowlock.

Hubris and Nemesis

Day and Leake, and indeed Fremantle, were able to bask in praise for their achievement.

At 2334 on 16 March the Admiralty sent to Beatty, 'Personal from First Sea Lord. I heartily congratulate you on your patient watch.' Beatty replied, 'Yr 440 appreciated. Will convey your commendation to those concerned.'

A more formal telegram followed on 20 March, copied to 2nd and 10th Cruiser Squadrons: 'The Board of Admiralty has learned with much satisfaction of the destruction of the German raider on the 16 March as the result of long and patient watch and successful dispositions.'

When the two triumphant vessels reached Scapa Flow two days after the battle, Rear Admiral Fremantle quickly came on board *Achilles* and addressed the crew, congratulating them on their success.

Day came in for personal praise. Fremantle wrote to Beatty as Commander-in-Chief Grand Fleet on 1 April:

> the vigilance exercised by this officer which caused him to suspect the status of the ship which he was boarding before sending away his boat, the judgement and ability with which he manoeuvred the *Dundee* to avoid torpedo attack and the promptitude with which he opened fire are desiring of the highest praise.

Fremantle went on to laud Lawson too:

> Hearing from his captain that he had suspicions as to the ship intercepted and knowing that the officer whose duty it was to board her had not any great experience, Lieutenant Lawson volunteered for the duty and lost his life as a consequence. I submit that the boarding of a craft already recognised as suspicious, when not in the course of his usual duty, is an action worthy of the highest honour.

Both Day and Leake, and their crews, could be forgiven for feeling pleased with themselves.

But vengeful fate was not long in taking the shine off the plaudits. On 23 March *Dundee* was on patrol with *Shannon*, a *Minotaur*-class armoured cruiser, a cousin rather than sister to *Achilles*. The weather was poor and getting worse when they spotted a three-masted barque. The sailing ship was ordered to heave to and Day inspected her closely, questioning her by signal. She was apparently *Eva*, on passage to Norway in ballast, and Norwegian-flagged. The weather conditions were now too poor to lower a boat to inspect her and Day expressed himself satisfied with *Eva*'s replies to his questions. *Eva* was allowed to proceed, and *Dundee* and *Shannon* resumed their patrols.

Three weeks later the *Frankfurter Zeitung* of 13 April carried a long piece about the escape from Chile of twenty-eight German sailors, once of the Hapag-Lloyd line, who, desperate to return to Germany to serve the Fatherland, had purchased an old sailing ship for 80,000 Chilean pesos. They sailed it halfway around the world until, reaching the Norwegian Sea, they were intercepted by British cruisers on 23 March. Pretending to be Norwegian, they made good an escape and arrived in Germany to a heroes' welcome. The newspaper article made much of how they had tricked the British blockade and proved the superiority of German prowess. It was, of course, *Eva*.

There was much embarrassment in the Admiralty at this propaganda coup. The Sea Lords sent a snorter of a letter, together with a translation of the offending article, to Fremantle and Tupper, demanding to know what had happened, and Fremantle in turn sent a stinker to Day and the captain of *Shannon*, Vincent Molteno. Abject apologies followed and Molteno subtly placed the blame on Day, whose assessment of the barque he had accepted. Shortly afterwards, a signal was sent to the 2nd and 10th Cruiser Squadrons to the effect that *all* intercepted ships should be boarded irrespective of the weather conditions, or stood to until weather permitted boarding or escorting to a British port.

Day remained in command of *Dundee* until June, when he was relieved, but the little steamer did not live long to enjoy her new fame. On 2 September she was sighted sailing off the Scilly Isles by *UC-49*. *Dundee* was torpedoed, and duly sank the next day with the loss of seven men: one an engineer sub lieutenant RNR and six MMR from the peacetime crew of the vessel. All the dead had been in the engine room when the torpedo struck.

PART FOUR

Endings

The story of the men and ships of the 10th and 2nd Cruiser Squadrons did not end with the despatch of *Leopard*. Nor did the suffering of the German people.

1 9

Secrets and Rewards

The war had become one in which every propaganda opportunity was taken to discredit the enemy or exaggerate success on the battlefield. Indeed, it was said of the British newspaper proprietor Lord Northcliffe, after the war was over, that 'the Germans ascribe their defeat and downfall largely to the effects of propaganda – mainly British – on their population and armies and that in the eyes of their High Command Lord Northcliffe himself was a general no less to be feared and respected than Foch'.

It is thus strange, indeed, that no opportunity was taken to publicise this rare success for the navy in home waters. The supply chain had been protected, an enemy sunk, and British and Commonwealth sailors had shown the required levels of pluck and sacrifice. But there was an official silence.

Six Andersons had served in the action and four had been killed. The *Shetland News* of 29 March gave the basic information that they had died – adding that they all had been in the pre-war RNR for between four and ten years, and were also seamen or fishermen. The *Shetland Times* too was nearly silent about the event; only a small entry in the Births, Marriages and Deaths column recorded the demise of Robert John Anderson (on 14 April 1917), Henry J (on 21 April 1917), Magnus John (also on 21 April 1917). There was no announcement for Henry. No mentions were made of the cause of their deaths. And the Adelaide *Chronicle* reported Frederick Lawson's death on 30 June 1917, stating that he was 'killed on active service on March 16th on HMS_____', the ship's name left blank.

Leake and Day's reports of the encounter were published by the *London Gazette* on 15 April 1919, six months after the war had ended. Indeed, it was only when *The Times* published a full report of the battle after the war (19 April 1919) that the Germans discovered what had happened to *Leopard*.

The news had spread to New Zealand by July 1919, a local paper reprinting *The Times* article and adding that that it was 'an action which was not reported at the time and but briefly announced sometime after'.

Why the silence? Was it a fear of giving too much information to the enemy as to the nature of the blockade and the type of ships operating it? The German unrestricted submarine campaign was at its height and Britain sorely needed good news. And yet the action went unremarked.

In 1915 Jacky Fisher, in a private letter to de Chair, had stated that 'you shall all be publicly praised but the fact is, strict secrecy is so necessary in the important work you are carrying out'. And de Chair himself had issued instructions, by memorandum to all commanding officers as early as February the same year, that the strictest reticence must be observed and that shore leave would be stopped if idle tongues blabbed when in port.

The officers involved in the blockade seemed not to know of the victory achieved by Leake and Day. The inveterate diary keeper Commander England noted in his diary entry of 17 March that 'a raider is said to have been seen yesterday away to the eastward', but makes no further reference to it or the successful sinking of *Leopard* in any entry up to December 1918. Nor does Captain Brocklebank's journal carry any information about the sighting or sinking of a raider around 16–17 March, or indeed any time thereafter.

Writing to his mother shortly after the action (26 March), Captain Leake noted:

My dear Mama. We came here yesterday and are now going on as usual. To get rid of our rat, on paper, was not a simple matter and caused me no small annoyance, they then asked for remains, however I now hope he is finally buried and that no interfering fool will dig him up. I am afraid I cannot produce any news however you have plenty from France and are lucky if you can keep up with it all. I cannot here.

Given that the letter was written only eight days after the event it is remarkable in two ways. First, that Leake states that he has no news to pass on, despite his recent success. Secondly, the description of 'the rat'. Is this a code for the disposal of *Leopard*? Is he passing on a message in some private code; it seems a little elaborate for the quotidian task of rat-catching on board ship. Leake, it seems, was bound to silence about their activities.

The answer appears to be that the Admiralty were very concerned that any sort of news about ship losses and successes would materially aid the enemy. Their view was summed up by Senator George Foster Pearce in the Australian parliament, where he was acting prime minister and minister for defence:

> the Admiralty has affirmed that the Central Powers are frequently ignorant concerning the losses of British and neutral vessels and also *the activities of their own vessels* [author's emphasis] ... the Navy Board is of the opinion that publication of losses of specific ships would ... convey to the enemy direct information regarding their activities and thus be of assistance to his operations.

The gain in propaganda was deemed to be outweighed by the provision of intelligence to the German navy.

Recognition and Reward
Despite the secrecy, the Admiralty was prepared to recognise and reward the efforts of *Achilles* and *Dundee*.

Commander Day was given the signal honour for a merchant service RNR of promotion to the rank of captain, with seniority backdated to the date of the action with *Leopard*. He was also awarded the Distinguished Service Order (DSO) on 22 June, although this was not published in the *London Gazette* until after the war. Captain Leake was also awarded the DSO and again not gazetted until 1919. His award noted that: 'His good judgement in dealing with the situation, and promptitude in opening heavy fire immediately the circumstances required it, undoubtedly averted loss or damage to the *Dundee*, which was engaging a ship with an armament considerably superior to her own.'

Day had particularly praised his gunlayers in his official report and recommended them for recognition. He noted:

> I desire to submit the names of the following Gunlayers: W Lee, PO1, RFR, J M Cullen, AB, RNVR (another Liverpudlian), J L Arthurson, Ldg Sea, RNR; J G Anderson, Sea, RNR for favourable consideration, because with no Officers of Quarters available ... they calmly and skilfully controlled the guns' crews and their own firing, doing their own spotting and judging point of aim to the most vital places about the raider's decks and hull, so that the enemy, who was approximately three times our size, complement and armament, was made by their marksmanship incapable of inflicting the smallest damage to us within the same period. In fact, the enemy ship at this time was stopped, disabled, and in time would have been entirely consumed by the fire then raging.

Beatty and the Admiralty concurred. Arthurson and Lee received the Distinguished Service Medal (DSM) while Anderson (second cousin to the deceased Henry) and Cullen were mentioned in despatches. Acting Lieutenant Lawson was posthumously given the same award, which was gazetted on 27 June 1917.

Leake preferred to acknowledge the contribution of two of his key officers. Lieutenant Commander Eustace Long, gunnery control officer, was mentioned in despatches, as was his navigating officer, Lieutenant Commander Albert Robertson, who was also 'noted for early promotion', having been praised by his captain as 'an exceptionally skilful and cool Navigating Officer'.

The dead found their recognition in small things. Frederick Lawson, who died so far from his home in South Australia, did not even merit a mention on Australia's national Roll of Honour. He does, however, gain a place on his country's Commemorative Roll which records the names of those Australians who died during war, but who were not serving in the Australian Armed Forces and therefore not eligible for inclusion on the Roll of Honour. The

Commemorative Roll has its own space in the Australian National War Memorial. And like all those who fell in the service of the navy, he has his name on one of the three great Royal Naval memorials, in this case at Portsmouth.

Widnes-born, Liverpool-based RNVR Able Seaman Alfred Birchall, 34-year-old husband of Florence, has his place on the Plymouth naval memorial, and in his home town of Bootle, where he is commemorated at Christ Church and on the Civic Roll of Honour.

All of the Andersons are recorded on the Shetland Islands Roll of Honour. Henry is also remembered on the savagely beautiful Whalsey Great War memorial.

J J Haldane Burgess (1862–1927), the Shetland poet and language scholar, remembered all of them, and more, when he wrote the introduction to the Shetland Roll of Honour in 1920:

Silent ye lie in distant lands and seas,
Heroes, whose names we trace with love and pride
Endless our debt to you, who fought and died,
That we might taste the sweets of life and ease.
Long shall the voice of fame your deeds recall,
And glory gild your names on storied page,
Noble and brave as in the sea-kings' age,
Defenders of fair freedom for us all.
High on the shining scroll of bright renown,
Emblazoned in the work wrought by your hands,
Refulgent now the name of Shetland stands,
On through long ages to be handed down:
Ever shall thoughts of your victorious strife
Stir Shetland's sons to greater, grander life.

20

Postscript

After the sinking of *Leopard*, the German navy never again attempted to use AMCs to raid British commerce. But it did make one more attempt at trade interdiction on the surface, this time using fast, modern naval forces.

On 16 October 1917 a convoy of twelve merchant ships, with two Royal Navy destroyers – *Mary Rose* and *Strongbow* – as escort, sailed from Norway with war materials for Britain. In the half-light of dawn the following day, seventy miles east of Lerwick, Lieutenant Commander Charles Leonard Fox, in command of *Mary Rose*, observed two warships approaching. Their profiles and dark-grey colour led him to assume they were British light cruisers, and recognition signals were transmitted. In fact they were a task force of German light cruisers, *Brummer* and *Bremse*.

In the confusion of the sighting, the German ships were able to close to less than 3,000yds before opening fire, quickly disabling *Strongbow*. After ensuring that all confidential papers had been destroyed, her captain ordered the surviving crew to abandon ship. *Mary Rose*, which had been ahead of the convoy, and only realised that the convoy was under attack when her crew heard gunfire, turned to fight but it was a total mismatch: the German ships were armed with eight 15cm (5.9in) guns between them, whilst the British destroyer could respond with only three 4in guns.

Mary Rose was hit in the engine room and crippled shortly after firing on her began. Sub Lieutenant Marsh RNVR maintained fire with the one gun left operational, while the only two surviving members of the torpedo crew were able to fire the last remaining torpedo, which missed. But it was a futile effort at self-defence;

further German salvoes wrecked the little unarmoured vessel and Fox ordered Gunner Isaac Hancock to scuttle the ship. The ship's boats had been reduced to splinters by German fire and only a handful of men were able to survive by clinging to a raft; Fox went down with the ship. Several hours later, the survivors boarded a lifeboat from one of the merchant ships and were eventually able to reach Norway. With the escorts disposed of, the German light cruisers were able to sink at leisure nine of the twelve-ship convoy.

Neither British destroyer had managed to make a radio report of the attack and the two German cruisers escaped unscathed, despite the presence of British cruiser forces in the area. Forty-six of *Strongbow*'s crew were killed in the attack, with thirty-six survivors, including her captain, Lieutenant Commander Edward Brooke, who nonetheless later died of pneumonia as a result of the action. But the difficulties of refuelling his ships due to the British blockade led Scheer, the German naval head, to discontinue his plan for further such operations and the surface raiders left the field once more to the U-boat. They would never again venture out.

* * *

Between March and June 1918 the Northern Patrol was replaced by a static minefield, stretching for 240 miles from the Orkneys to Hardanger Fjord. The objective was now different. U-boat egress was the issue, a task that the original patrol had never been intended to undertake. The central area was laid by the American navy and was itself 130 miles long. Overall, the minefield was not a success, for the U-boats it was intended to catch simply went round it through Norwegian territorial waters. There was some talk from the Americans and others of coercing the Norwegians to lay their own mines, thus completing the closure of the passage. Beatty, now Commander-in-Chief Grand Fleet at Scapa, would have none of this. In total, despite the massive expenditure on mines and vessels, the new field accounted for only four to six U-boats sunk.

At no time did Britain suffer the collapse of food and other supplies that affected Germany and the morale of her people. Although rationing was eventually introduced in Britain in 1918 (*vide supra*), the necessary calorie intake was consistently exceeded and there was no adverse consequence for the health of the nation.

Nevertheless, there was a time in 1917 when it was a close-run thing. Germany's onslaught on British supply lines through unrestricted submarine warfare had the dual effect of removing necessary cargo tonnage from the overall merchant fleet (through sinkings and damage) and preventing the safe arrival (or sometimes despatch) of food and other commodities. Shipbuilding could not keep pace with losses and the Admiralty despaired that there would be insufficient merchant ship capacity for the cargo tonnage necessary for Britain's survival.

As has been described earlier, the first attempt on British trades was primarily through AMCs (generally, converted liners) during 1914 and early 1915. The emphasis then turned to unrestricted submarine warfare, until American outrage caused the withdrawal of the U-boats in March 1916. Raiders such as *Moewe* and *Leopard* now came again to the fore. The final stage was the unrestricted submarine warfare declared at the beginning of February 1917 and which lasted until the war's end. This book is primarily about surface raiders, but note must be made of the impact of German undersea warfare in 1917 and the solution to it adopted.

In the war months of 1914, British merchant tonnage sunk amounted to 241,000 tons or an annualised rate of 576,000 tons. In 1915, total losses were 855,000 tons; and in 1916, 1,237,000 tons. These rates of loss were significant but not critical. However, in 1917 losses totalled 3,729,785 tons. The impact on the monthly losses due to the advent of the unrestricted campaign in February 1917 can be seen in the following table.

Month	Tons lost
Oct 1916	176,248
Nov 1916	168,809
Dec 1916	182,292
Jan 1917	153,666
Feb 1917	313,486
Mar 1917	353,478
Apr 1917	545,282
May 1917	352,289

With such a level of losses, new shipbuilding could not keep pace. Jellicoe, First Sea Lord, became despondent at the prospect of ending the submarine threat, and political and public concern at the navy's inability to stem the tide of losses grew.

The answer was staring the Sea Lords in the face – convoy, a proven vehicle for containing losses in many previous wars. Indeed, the thirteenth-century Venetians used convoy and armed escort for their trade with Flanders and the Levant; they called it the *muda* system. But the Royal Navy was reluctant to adopt convoy. For this there were three overriding reasons.

First, convoy was seen as a defensive measure, an admission that the much vaunted Royal Navy could not master its enemies. It went against the navy's view of itself as an aggressive, attacking force which hunted the seas for its prey and won manly battles against them. The passive nature of convoy and escort did not appeal to the navy's *amour propre*.

Secondly, many admirals – and Jellicoe in particular – were worried about the lack of numbers of destroyers and light cruisers which were necessary for convoy escort duty and which would have to be taken from the Grand Fleet (especially) to provide the needful amount of escorts. Jellicoe and others still saw that the role of the Grand Fleet was to seek out the Imperial High Seas Fleet in battle, if it could ever be tempted to come out, and destroy it. For this, the light cruisers and destroyers were seen as essential to the Fleet's objective, and Jellicoe and Beatty were reluctant to let them go to the 'defensive' role of convoy escort.

Thirdly, due to a misreporting and misunderstanding of the number of ship movements that would have to be covered by convoy, the Sea Lords felt that the totality of the task was beyond the capability of the ships on hand to undertake.

It might also be noted that shipowners were also often unenthusiastic towards convoy; one of the reasons for the 1872 repeal of the Compulsory Convoys Act had been the view that convoys were obsolete because of the increased speeds of merchant ships. Some shipowners still preferred to take their own chances against commerce raiders rather than wait for convoys to be formed, on the basis that time was money.

As the correct information emerged and a more utilitarian view of convoy developed in the face of public opinion, the Royal Navy edged towards the introduction of a convoy system. Lloyd George, prime minister since his 'coup' at the end of 1916, took credit for the change, and it is true that he stormed over to the Admiralty in person to demand of Jellicoe and his political boss Sir Edward Carson that they introduce convoy immediately. But the necessary change of mindset had, in fact, already taken place, assisted by the entry of America into the war and the consequent need to transport large numbers of troops across the Atlantic. The results were instantaneous. Convoy was introduced on 24 May 1917 and, as the table below demonstrates, immediately reduced the rate of loss.

Month	Tons lost
July 1917	364,858
Aug 1917	329,810
Sept 1917	196,212
Oct 1917	276,132
Nov 1917	173,560
Dec 1917	253,087
Jan 1918	179,973
Feb 1918	226,898
Mar 1918	199,458

Convoy saved the day! And this was a solution unavailable to the Germans, for they could neither get escort vessels out from their home bases to find incoming ships, nor fight them through the Northern and Southern Blockades without the certainty of heavy and unsustainable losses (nor did they now have access to a merchant fleet of any significance).

The fallacy of the belief that aggressive hunting-down of U-boats was a better answer was exposed when the Northern Patrol was reconstituted briefly in 1918 to seek and kill submarines evading the mine barrage (which had replaced the standing patrols) in the Fair Isle channel. They caught exactly none.

As for surface raiders, over the course of the whole war they sank 442,702 tons of British merchant tonnage; out of a total of

7,759,090 tons, submarines accounted for 6,635,059. Mines did more damage than surface raiders, at 673,417 tons.

* * *

Shortly after the action with *Leopard*, Leake was promoted to commodore second-class and chief of staff to the Commander-in-Chief Western Approaches, Admiral Sir Lewis Bayly. An unbending man with several chips on his shoulders, Bayly could be difficult to work for, but Leake mastered him, and their partnership became one of great respect, more so after the Americans entered the war and Bayly took charge of American anti-submarine forces based at Queenstown. Through force of personality, the British pair made themselves hugely respected by their American allies. Bayly later wrote of Leake, 'a most exceptional man, for everyone loved the little Commodore'.

Promotion to rear admiral followed and in mid-1919 he left Ireland to take up the post of chief of staff to Vice Admiral Sir Henry F Oliver, Vice Admiral Commanding the Home Fleet, which in November became the Reserve Fleet. He retired in 1921, was appointed a Companion of the Bath (CB) and awarded the US navy's Distinguished Service Medal. But he did not enjoy good health in retirement. He died at his family home of Marshalls in Hertfordshire on 21 January 1928, after a three-year illness, aged only fifty-nine; he was buried in St John the Evangelist Churchyard, High Cross. The cause of death was given as 'dementia paralytica', a diagnosis generally used for the tertiary phase of syphilis.

Bayly wrote his *Times* obituary:

Although Vice Admiral Martin Leake was very little known outside the Service, it is true to say that no officer of or near his standing was so highly respected and more universally liked in the Navy than he was ... During his service as Chief of Staff in Queenstown he made a great reputation and friendship among the United States officers and men owing to his selfless tact and constant willingness to help all ranks and ratings of whatever nationality.

Captain Selwyn M Day received another rare honour when he was appointed a naval aide-de-camp to King George V on 1 February 1921, an unheard-of distinction for a RNR officer. He retired in 1922, became a member of the Society for Nautical Research, was appointed secretary of the Sea Lion training ship *London* and emigrated to Australia in 1932, settling in Sydney. There he wrote various books, including *Australia's Imminent Peril* (published in 1934) and articles on naval matters including 'Australia's Need for a Sea Training System' in 1933 (which resulted in a clutch of letters to the papers). He was an advocate for the training of boys to be seamen through service on sail training ships and submitted a scheme for the training of Australian boys for sea careers to the New South Wales government in 1936. It was rejected. His patriotism for his new country led him to say, in a 1937 address to the Young Citizens Association, that 'Australia's defences are unique and tragic.' Day died in August 1938 aged sixty-five, married but childless.

Frederick Lawson's family did not forget him. Two years after his death, the *Adelaide Chronicle* carried no less than five *in memoria*, in the Family Notices section, under the column Heroes of the Great War. His sister and brother-in-law, L and F Sincock (and baby Max) wrote, 'In loving memory of our dear brother Lieutenant Frederick Lawson RNR killed whilst doing his duty on HMS *Dundee*: We think of his life, a duty done / Manly, unselfish and brave'.

He was 'sadly missed' by his Aunt Elim, Uncle Alf and cousins in Birkenhead; missed by his 'loving grandma, Aunt Hettie and Aunt Hannah'; 'so dearly loved, so sadly missed' by his loving Aunt Till, Uncle Sam and cousins in Exeter; and his brother and sister-in-law, John, Beth and children, inserted: 'No token of love in that far off land / To mark the spot where he sleepeth now'.

The death of *Leopard* was immortalised in oils in 1920 by William Lionel Wyllie, the most distinguished marine artist of his day. His painting *The Destruction of the German raider Leopard by HMS Achilles and HMS Dundee*, is now owned by the Imperial War Museum (as is his painting of the loss of *Pathfinder*, executed in the same year).

Dudley de Chair was recalled from the Foreign Office in September 1917 and given command of the 3rd Battle Squadron at

Scapa. However, the dismissal of his friend Jellicoe from the post of First Sea Lord (on Christmas Eve, by letter) filled him with horror and he expressed himself forcibly to the new First Lord, Rosslyn Wemyss. As he wrote in his memoirs:

> A few days later, after Jellicoe had been so unjustly dismissed, and while my flagship was still coaling, I received an urgent telegram from Wemyss to go to the Admiralty. On arrival I was greeted warmly by him, but I was still boiling over with indignation about Jellicoe's dismissal, and the way Wemyss had betrayed him. When Wemyss began talking of filling vacancies at the Admiralty, and asked me to take one of the posts on the Board of Admiralty vacated by one of the admirals who had resigned in consequence of Jellicoe's dismissal, I told him that I would not and could not take a post at the Admiralty, as I felt so keenly the disgraceful manner in which Jellicoe had been treated. I added that I was surprised that any naval officer on the Board of Admiralty could remain there, as it looked as if they condoned this action of Jellicoe's dismissal. In fact, I expressed myself forcibly, and let myself go, and left him after a scene which did me no good and had disastrous results.

Perhaps unsurprisingly, he was asked to haul down his flag shortly afterwards and went on half-pay, to be appointed Admiral Commanding Coast Guards and Reserves – not a challenging or sea-going role – in July 1918.

De Chair's role in the blockade and starvation of Germany was recognised even within Germany itself. To celebrate the escape of *Moewe*, a bronze medal was struck which was sold on the streets of Berlin during the war. On one side it read '*Dem Britischen Vice Admiral Dudley de Chair Gewidmet*' (dedicated to Vice Admiral Dudley de Chair). On the obverse was a depiction of a seagull (*Moewe*), with a fish in its mouth, flying over and past two sea lions, representing the British blockade.

He was promoted admiral in November 1920, and in 1923, his royal connections and urbane personality no doubt playing a part in his selection, followed Belloc's Lord Lundy's example by being appointed governor of New South Wales, where he found the politicians, and especially Premier Lang, to be less than congenial. Lang's 'lack of scruple gave me a great and unpleasant surprise'.

He stood down in 1930, went on a world tour, wrote his memoirs and died in Brighton in 1958, aged ninety-three.

De Chair's flag captain aboard *Crescent* and *Alsatian* had been George Trewby. After de Chair's departure for Whitehall, Trewby left the squadron and took command of the armoured cruiser *Kent*. He too received belated recognition with the award of a CMG (Companion of the Order of St Michael and St George) in July 1919, 'for valuable services as Flag Captain and Chief of Staff to the Rear Admiral Commanding, 10th Cruiser Squadron'.

The 10th Cruiser Squadron, though disbanded in 1917, was not forgotten by those who had sailed with it. On 4 April 1931 a re-union dinner was held on board the (renamed) SS *Empress of France* (docked at Southampton), once the 10th Cruiser Squadron flagship *Alsatian*, presided over by de Chair, and attended by twelve admirals (including Admiral of the Fleet Sir Roger Keyes, Commander-in-Chief Portsmouth, and French Vice Admiral C Berthelot, Commander-in-Chief Cherbourg, who had captained *Champagne* on attachment to the 10th Cruiser Squadron) and rep-resentatives of all ships and liners which had served.

In a speech, de Chair recalled how Germany had struck a medal to 'the eternal damnation of him and the squadron'. He had asked the Foreign Office to obtain one for him and about the time he received it the German press reported that he was dead. His wife had received touching letters of sympathy!

He went on to explain the lack of awareness at home of the squadron's activities: 'The exploits of the squadron were never adequately reported owing to the necessity for the strictest secrecy. The Germans knew a jolly sight more about it than Britain.' In his speech, De Chair claimed that in 1915 alone the squadron had 'intercepted 3,100 ships of which 690 were sent to British ports under armed guard'.

And the *Official History of Naval Operations*, published in 1923, handsomely endorsed his position, noting for 1915 that:

During all this time, when our fleets were completely dominating the North Sea, the part which the 10th Cruiser

Squadron silently played in the shadow of the Grand Fleet must not be forgotten. It was still under the command of Rear Admiral D R S de Chair, and had reached its full complement of twenty-four armed merchant cruisers under Royal Navy captains. Undeterred by the incessant gales, in all but continuous darkness as the season advanced, and blinded with snow and fog, they held their ground. Uncomplaining and vigilant, the merchant seamen and officers who manned the ships kept their grip on the enemy's throat with no less spirit and resource than their comrades in the fleet.

The lessons of the 10th Cruiser Squadron were soon forgotten. When Britain and Germany were again at war in 1939, another Northern Patrol was instigated (under the command of Admiral Max Horton) and again used cruisers drawn from the reserve, which proved unable to stand up to the winter weather. By December they had been replaced by AMCs.

Reginald Tupper was awarded the KCB and mentioned in despatches for his time in the north, 'for services in 10th Cruiser Squadron which he commanded with much success'. After the war, he succeeded Bayly as Commander-in-Chief Queenstown and two years later retired to chair the council of the Royal United Services Institution. In 1933 at the age of seventy-three he married Caroline Maud Abadie, the widow of the quondam lieutenant governor of Jersey, his first wife having deceased in 1927, and in 1935 was awarded a service pension of £300 per annum (some £17,500 today). He died on 5 March 1945.

Captain Thomas Wardle of *Alcantara,* vanquisher of the *Greif,* survived his reprimand and went on to become rear admiral in command of the Australian fleet between April 1924 and April 1926, after which he stood down at his own request and was advanced to the rank of vice admiral on the retired list. George Bennett Weston Young of *Andes*, his partner in the action, joined the SNO Liverpool, Admiral Stileman, as his chief of staff, was promoted captain and received from the French the award of the *Croix d'Officer*, gazetted in September 1916. He died in 1941.

What of the quintet of diarists whose journals have illuminated the story of the 10th Cruiser Squadron (and in flagrant disregard for service regulations which prohibited an officer from keeping a private diary on active service whether ashore or afloat)? In July 1915 Alexander Scrimgeour was transferred to the battlecruiser *Invincible*, flagship of Rear Admiral Horace Hood. Scrimgeour had been identified as someone with potential and the transfer was intended to be a forcing house for him. Appointed acting sub lieutenant and given a position of responsibility in one of the main gun turrets as officer in charge X-turret, he died on 31 May 1916 at Jutland alongside nearly all his crewmates, when *Invincible* blew up under fire from two German capital ships. There were six survivors.

Ernest Lionel McKeag left the navy and the sea with the rank of sub lieutenant RNR, never to return, perhaps understandably given his near-death in the cold seas off Norway. He became a jobbing writer, turning out deathless prose for comics such as *The Magnet* under a variety of pseudonyms.

John Allen Shuter left *Changuinola* on 9 June 1915 to join a squadron of paddle steamers engaged in minesweeping. He confided to his diary 'left ship at 7 am. I have only once been so sorry to leave a ship before'. He retired in December 1920 from *Crescent* with the rank of commander. His cricketing father had died a month before his retirement and left him his collection of *Wisden*s. Shuter re-enlisted in 1939 for the next war, commanding anti-submarine trawlers and armed yachts, and died in 1974 at the Royal Navy's Haslar Hospital, aged eighty-seven years old.

George Plunkett England was appointed to the rank of captain in 1917, and after the war commanded an old battleship and two cruisers before retirement in 1921. His beloved daughter Margaret (Margy) married in 1935 another naval officer, William A Dallmeyer, who was to win the DSO for sinking a German submarine in 1941 and would rise to the rank of commodore. England died in 1957, at the age of eighty.

Henry Cyril Royds Brocklebank lost his brother Ralph on the Western Front in 1917, gained the rank of captain and in January 1918 became the naval attaché in Sweden, his experiences inter-cepting that country's ships no doubt proving invaluable in the role. He was made a CBE for his war service and retired to the life of a country gentleman in Dorset, buying and selling farm estates around Donhead St Mary. He died in June 1957, aged eighty-three, having served as a local justice of the peace, been awarded a DL, and married his daughter to the son of an admiral.

Possibly the most interesting career was that of Francis Grenfell. After service in *Cedric*, Grenfell volunteered for Q-ships and won the DSO and bar for the sinking of two German submarines in 1916 and 1917, gaining promotion to captain on the retired list as well. Demobilised on 25 November 1918, he immediately returned to the Board of Education and also gained recognition as a climber and mountaineer (and a founder member of the Climbers' Club) of repute. Retiring from the board aged sixty, he began training as a sculptor at the London Polytechnic and within eighteen months had his works accepted by the Royal Academy. A noted collector of British etchings, he never married and died, aged seventy-one, in 1946.

Of the Royal Navy captains who vanquished the German converted liners, Noel Grant was given command of the old *Warrior*-class cruiser *Cochrane* in June 1915, but he was not a well man and was found medically unfit for sea duty in February 1916, having contracted severe pneumonia, 'largely bought about by his experiences on the *Carmania*'; he was moved to command a shore establishment. In January 1920 he was promoted rear admiral on his retirement and died of a recurrence of pneumonia after a severe operation for appendicitis only six weeks later, aged only fifty-one. Captain James Barr, who had been *Carmania*'s peacetime commander, returned to Cunard as commodore of the fleet, retired on health grounds in 1916 and, unlike his erstwhile colleague, lived to the ripe old age of eighty-two.

The conqueror of *Kaiser Wilhelm der Grosse*, Henry Tritton Buller, enjoyed a full and prosperous career, attaining flag rank and being appointed to the gilded position of Admiral Commanding the Royal Yachts in 1922, a position he was to hold for the next ten years. In 1932 he became groom-in-waiting to the King, and in this position he was to serve no less than four monarchs, George V, Edward VIII, George VI and Elizabeth II, until his death at the age of eighty-seven in 1960.

Captain Bisset Smith's stepson, Alfred, had been taken prisoner by the Germans after the action with *Moewe* and spent twenty-one months in a POW camp, latterly working as a hospital orderly.

When finally released, he was said to be 'in a very weak state of health', and was given a post at the Admiralty in London.

In 1936 some of Bisset Smith's relatives presented the Otaki Shield to the governors of Robert Gordon's College, Aberdeen, where he had been educated, to be awarded annually to the scholar judged pre-eminent in character, leadership and athletics.

From 1938, the New Zealand Shipping Company added a travel scholarship in the form of a return trip to New Zealand – a tradition which continued when they were taken over, with P&O providing the passage.

In March 1951 Captain Bisset Smith's VC was bought at auction by the New Zealand Shipping Company and for two years it was housed in Robert Gordon's College, then placed in a 'new' *Otaki* when it was built in 1953. It remained in the officers' dining room until *Otaki* was sold in 1975. The medal then passed into the possession of P&O, where it was displayed in the office of the chairman.

Nikolaus Dohna-Schlodien was appointed a naval aide to the Kaiser in May 1918 and, at the end of the war, took command of a *Freikorps* (a militia formed from ex-soldiers to counter the revolutionary communist and Spartakus left wing uprisings) during what was effectively a civil war in Germany. He retired from the navy in 1919 and worked as a merchant in Hamburg before moving to Baierbach in the 1930s. He married Hilde von Laffert (née von Reichenau), the widow of his good friend Hans von Laffert, who had died on *Leopard* on 16 March 1917. Hilde, who was ten years younger than her new husband, had one daughter from her previous marriage, Marion von Laffert. Nikolaus and Hilde had two more daughters together, Hildegarde and Margaret. He died in 1956, holding the distinction of being one of only two German officers of the First World War who received the highest military awards of all five of the main German states: Pour le Mérite (Prussia); Military Order of Max Joseph (Bavaria); Military Order of St Henry (Saxony); Military Merit Order (Württemberg); Military Karl-Friedrich Merit Order (Baden); Iron Cross of 1914, 1st and 2nd class.

Two of von Laffet's siblings achieved fame in other fields, his elder brother Karl August as a science-fiction writer and his sister

Viktoria (under her married name of von Dirksen) as an inter-war *salonnière* who promoted Hitler into aristocratic society.

*   *   *

Achilles was transferred to the North America and West Indies station in August 1917 for convoy escort duties, but returned to Britain for a refit between February and December 1918. Upon completion of this she became a stokers' training ship at Chatham. In February 1919 the *London Gazette* announced her (and *Dundee*'s) prize money for the sinking of *Leopard* and, hopelessly obsolete by the war's end, she was sold for scrap in May 1921.

The antiquated *Edgar*-class cruisers with which de Chair had manfully tried to establish the blockade in 1914, and which had proved so unfitted to the task, were relegated to lesser duties.

Four of the class, *Edgar*, *Theseus*, *Endymion* and *Grafton*, were modified for service in the Dardanelles fiasco as bombardment or shore support vessels by the addition of anti-torpedo bulges, minesweeping gear over the bow and extra stiffening on the hull sides. The 9.2in guns were also replaced by single 6in guns with the removed guns being fitted in M15-class monitors. They ended the war in the Aegean. Between July 1915 and August 1917 *Grafton* was commanded by Captain Henry Edgar ('Dasher') Grace, son of the legendary cricketer W G.

Gibraltar, as has been narrated, became a depot ship for the 10th Cruiser Squadron at Swarbacks Minn. *St George* also became a depot ship, as did de Chair's former flagship, *Crescent*, for submarines, a fate also assigned to *Royal Arthur*.

Immediately the war ended, they were all laid up and were sold for scrap between 1920 and 1921, except *Gibraltar*, which survived until 1923. These old ladies had been built in another age and for another type of war. Nobody wanted them now.

After the war the German navy named a new torpedo boat *Leopard*; launched in 1928, she was christened by Hans von Laffert's daughter, Marion. In the Second World War she was accidentally rammed by the minelayer *Kaiser* and sunk.

Moewe was brought back into service in the Baltic as a submarine tender, before becoming the auxiliary minelayer *Ostsee* in 1918. At the war's end she went to Britain as reparations and was operated by Elders and Fyffes as the freighter *Greenbrier*, back in the banana trade. In 1933 she was sold to a German shipping company, and as the freighter *Oldenburg* was used to carry cargo between Germany and occupied Norway in the Second World War. On 7 April 1945, at the very end of the European war, she was attacked by Bristol Beaufighters of RAF Coastal Command on anti-shipping missions off the Norwegian coast. Holed by their rockets and strafed by cannon fire, she burned and sank.

Following the sinking of *Leopard*, the Germans had abandoned the idea of surface raiders and focussed on the undersea war, with initially devastating effect. Only the adoption of convoy, forced on a reluctant Royal Navy through parliamentary pressure and mounting ship and cargo losses, stemmed the tide. But the British and Allied blockade never faltered. Germany was literally starving when the armistice was signed.

In December 1918 the National Health Office in Berlin calculated that, by then, 763,000 persons had died as a result of the blockade; the number added to this in the first months of 1919 was never calculated. The armistice saw the intensification of the suffering, since the German Baltic coast was now effectively blockaded and German fishing rights in the Baltic annulled.

The military terms imposed by the triumphant Allies were hard. The German army was made to give up large amounts of weapons, to hand over raw materials and rail equipment and immediately evacuate occupied territory; the fleet was to be interned. German territory on the left bank of the Rhine was to be occupied by the Allies and Alsace-Lorraine returned to the French. But these conditions might be considered appropriate for a beaten foe which had sought an end to the fighting. The civilian terms were harsher. The British naval blockade was to continue and although some help was grudgingly provided with limited food supplies, the German peoples were to be kept hungry; part revenge perhaps, part to keep the nation subjugated and part necessity, as the French in particular had their own food supply problems to solve first. Command of the sea allowed the victorious Allies command of the supply chain. Erzberger, one of the German negotiators, gave notice that the civilian terms of the armistice would drive Germany to anarchy and famine; in this he was not incorrect.

In early March 1919 General Herbert Plumer, commander of the British Army of Occupation, informed Prime Minister Lloyd George that his men were begging to be sent home; 'they could no longer stand the sight of hordes of skinny and bloated children pawing over the offal from the British camps'.

Some journalists welcomed the situation. One wrote of the tens of thousands of Germans now in the wombs of famished mothers who 'are destined for a life of physical inferiority'.

Altogether, in all waters, seventeen armed merchant cruisers were lost (out of sixty-five which served), fourteen of them to torpedo attack, ten when with the Northern Patrol. A further three merchantmen, deployed as armed escorts, were also lost to submarines (out of a total of fourteen in service). Thirty-eight armed boarding steamers were commissioned, of which twelve were lost, including *Dundee*, nine of them to torpedoes. Two Northern Patrol armed trawlers were also sunk out of eighteen deployed.

In total, the 10th Cruiser Squadron, during the period of its existence (approximately forty-one months) had intercepted 8,905 ships, sent 1,816 into port under armed guard, and boarded a further 4,520 fishing craft.

The 10th and 2nd Cruiser Squadrons, the Northern Blockade, the RNR, RFR and RNVR men who crewed them, the Shetlanders who supported them, the obsolescent armoured cruisers, the ungainly AMCs – they were a polyglot force to throw against the Kaiser's navy. But they did the job. If the war was eventually won on the Western Front, the victory was in no small part due to the unsung work of this composite force and the psychological effect of their efforts on a German housewife's kitchen, whilst British kitchens produced no such angst. As the distinguished historian Arthur Marder noted, 'The growing demoralisation of the [German] home front in 1918 caused by blockade, and which culminated in a revolutionary outbreak, had given the *coup de grâce* to the German military effort.'

Britain's vital supply lines were kept clear of surface raiders and Germany's trades were successfully, and almost completely, interdicted. The Royal Navy may not have won a new Trafalgar; it may have suffered a number of wasteful and avoidable losses; but, in the end, with its foot on the neck of its enemy, the Royal Navy won the only battle that really mattered – that of the command of the seas.

Admiral Sir David Beatty knew this when, near the end of the war, he wrote in a paper of 23 October regarding terms for an armistice:

> The Military successes have been great and the Military Terms are commensurate with their achievements. The Navy made them possible and therefore shares in them. The Navy also has won a great Passive Victory, has swept the Enemy from the seas, and rendered secure the vast lines of communication with our Allies and permitted the trade of this country, necessary for existence to continue. Because ours is a Passive Victory, it is no reason why the Empire should not reap the fruits of that victory.

The historian C R M F Cruttwell endorsed this view. Writing in 1934 he noted that:

> the rigour of the blockade made food more and more difficult to obtain and less palatable, deprived the young of milk and fats and enormously increased the deaths of infants and tuberculous persons. The whole country was growing out-at-elbows. Almost every article that could be bought was a dingy or repellent substitute for the original.

And Prime Minister Lloyd George, looking back on the time from a 1930s vantage point, remained convinced of the contribution that the navy had brought to the Allied success in the Great War. 'Our own Generals ... could have no armies on any battlefield had it not been for the compete command of the sea which our sailors, and their auxiliary helpers on shore, succeeded in maintaining; and the British people would have been driven to make peace in order to avert famine.' In this view he was supported by two other statesmen of the war cabinet, Andrew Bonar Law, who, the day after Armistice Day, remarked in the House of Commons that 'the downfall of the military colossus was due to blockade, which had sapped the whole foundation of Germany'; and A J Balfour, who noted that 'the labours of the 10th Cruiser Squadron were more continuous, more important and more successful than any other branch of His Majesty's Naval Forces'.

But perhaps the final word should reflect the contribution that men like Lieutenant Lawson, Captain Leake, Commander Day, the Andersons and their like made to the British success at arms, together with the 50,000 merchant marine sailors and 4,500 merchant ships and fishing vessels which were requisitioned for the war effort. As the *Daily Mail* stated in 1919: 'The main advantage which we possessed over the Germans lay in the character, the seamanship and the courage of our seamen.'

2 1

Coda

This is the fourth book that I have written about the Royal Navy in the First World War. The many people who have encouraged my efforts in writing these books have oft times urged me to pick more 'commercial' topics to explore. But the period and the Royal Navy hold a fascination for me.

The Great War marked a demarcation point between ages. Before, in the 'Vicwardian' age of gilded splendour, massive scientific and industrial advance and imperial dominion, there was a certainty of position in the world, of merit or otherwise, and of a structure and demarcation of society that had been largely unchanged for centuries. If one had money, it was undoubtedly the best time of all history to be alive; and if one wanted money and had the energy and idea to make something happen, it was the best time to make money.

The aristocracy still dominated society and governance, but increasingly, men of commerce were entering the lists too. And the upper classes' contribution to the maintenance of society was seen as a duty: it was not paid, not expecting of much material reward, and certainly not the venal and morally corrupt governing class that we are fettered with today. The great government under Lord Salisbury of 1895–1902 can possibly be reckoned to be the last 'disinterested' government that Britain has had.

The Royal Navy reflected society at large except, as a closed system, perhaps more so. Officers came from the landed or aristocratic classes, promotion from the lower class was almost impossible. But it also possessed the same disinterested quality;

heroism was expected, one was meant to recognise that to lay down one's life in the service of the Empire was a good – and sometimes necessary – thing. Self-sacrifice and the protection of those less able to protect themselves was an unwritten rule.

All this was changed by the First World War; the world left behind was an uncertain, more cynical, more grasping world than that which had obtained beforehand. Those times have gone and can never be recaptured. And that is, I suspect, the attraction of such TV programmes as *Downton Abbey* and such books as those of P G Wodehouse, and the sublime music of Edward Elgar. I like to imagine John Shuter, in his lonely piano practice, playing Elgar. Perhaps it was *In Smyrna,* inspired by a Mediterranean cruise Elgar took with his friend Frank Schuster in the autumn of 1905 aboard the Royal Navy ship *Surprise.** The naval connection would make it a perfect fit.

So that is my first reason for writing about the period, the desire to understand and portray a forgotten and, to my mind, more attractive past.

The second reason is more scientific. The First World War at sea used weapons which are recognisable, in many cases almost unchanged, today in the twenty-first century. But the strategic thinking was largely eighteenth- or, at best, nineteenth-century in its execution. I wanted to understand what made the men who fought the war act as they did; and what cultural, educational and societal influences formed their world view and mindset.

Thus my books focus more on the men than on the materiel. On the ways that their acts seemed to them or to their peers. On their quotidian heroism.

It seems to me that there was an almost fatalistic acceptance of their situation and an assumption that heroic behaviour was the norm; men of all stations went through the severest of ordeals and yet appeared not to regard it as anything other than their duty or their lot. Heroism or bravery was simply what a man did and to let the side down was worse than treachery.

---

* *Surprise* was then commanded by Commander Edward F Bruen, who – as a rear admiral – succeeded Tupper as commanding officer of the 2nd Cruiser Squadron on 21 February 1918.

The values that they represented – honour, loyalty, obedience, bravery, sacrifice – came to be derided; now they are lost for ever through a changed political and educational prism which makes it difficult for us today to wholly comprehend their actions. I wanted to understand them, report them and hopefully show my readers this very different world to the one we now live in. I hope that I have been, over the course of the four books, successful.

Mere ships do not make a fleet, nor do they form the right arm of an empire; for the strength of an empire does not lie in armour guns and torpedoes, but in the souls of the men behind these things.**

** General Kuropatkin, Russian Commander-in-Chief Russo-Japanese war of 1904–1905.

APPENDIX 1

Moewe's Victims

Ships sunk or captured by *Moewe* on her first raiding voyage

Date	Ship	Type	Nationality	Tonnage grt	Fate
11 Jan 16	*Corbridge*	Cargo ship	UK	3,687	Retained as prize; scuttled 30 Jan 16
11 Jan 16	*Farringford*	Cargo ship	UK	3,146	Sunk
13 Jan 16	*Dromonby*	Cargo ship	UK	3,627	Sunk
13 Jan 16	*Author*	Cargo ship	UK	3,496	Sunk
13 Jan 16	*Trader*	Cargo ship	UK	3,608	Sunk
15 Jan 16	*Ariadne*	Cargo ship	UK	3,035	Sunk
15 Jan 16	*Appam*	Cargo ship	UK	7,781	Retained as prize; detached 17 Jan 16; returned 28 Mar 17
16 Jan 16	*Clan McTavish*	Cargo ship	UK	5,816	Sunk in action
22 Jan 16	*Edinburgh*	Sailing ship	UK	1,473	Sunk
4 Feb 16	*Luxembourg*	Cargo ship	UK	4,322	Sunk
6 Feb 16	*Flamenco*	Cargo ship	UK	4,540	Sunk
8 Feb 16	*Westburn*	Cargo ship	UK	3,300	Retained as prize; detached 9 Feb 16
9 Feb 16	*Horace*	Cargo ship	UK	3,109	Sunk
24 Feb 16	*Maroni*	Cargo ship	UK	3,109	Sunk
25 Feb 16	*Saxon Prince*	Cargo ship	UK	3,471	Sunk

Sunk by mines from *Moewe* on her first raiding voyage

Date	Ship	Type	Nationality	Tonnage grt	Location
6 Jan 16	*King Edward VII*	Pre-dreadnought battleship	UK Royal Navy	16,350 (displacement)	Scotland
13 Jan 16	*Bayo*	Cargo ship	Spain	2,776	Gironde
13 Jan 16	*Belgica*	Cargo ship	Spain	2,068	Gironde

193

Ships sunk or captured by *Moewe*, sailing as *Vineta* on her second raiding voyage

Date	Ship	Type	Nationality	Tonnage grt	Fate
27 Jul 16	*Eskimo*	Cargo ship	UK	3,326	Taken as a prize

Ships sunk or captured by *Moewe* on her third raiding voyage

Date	Ship	Type	Nationality	Tonnage grt	Fate
2 Dec 16	*Voltaire*	Cargo ship	UK	8,618	Sunk
4 Dec 16	*Hallbjørg*	Cargo ship	UK	2,586	Sunk
6 Dec 16	*Mount Temple*	Cargo ship	UK	9,792	Sunk
8 Dec 16	*Duchess of Cornwall*	Sailing ship	UK	152	Sunk
8 Dec 16	*King George*	Cargo ship	UK	3,852	Sunk
9 Dec 16	*Cambrian Range*	Cargo ship	UK	4,235	Sunk
10 Dec 16	*Georgic*	Cargo ship	UK	10,077	Sunk
11 Dec 16	*Yarrowdale*	Cargo ship	UK	4,652	Retained as prize; detached to Swinemunde, 31 Dec 16. Converted to auxiliary cruiser *Leopard*
12 Dec 16	*Saint Theodore*	Cargo ship	UK	4,992	Commissioned as auxiliary cruiser *Geier*; scuttled 14 Feb 17
18 Dec 16	*Dramatist*	Cargo ship	UK	5,415	Sunk
26 Dec 16	*Nantes*	Sailing ship	UK	2,679	Sunk
2 Jan 17	*Asnières*	Sailing ship	UK	3,103	Sunk
5 Jan 17	*Hudson Maru*	Cargo ship	Japan	3,798	Sunk
8 Jan 17	*Radnorshire*	Cargo ship	UK	4,310	Sunk
9 Jan 17	*Minteh*	Cargo ship	UK	2,890	Sunk
10 Jan 17	*Netherby Hall*	Cargo ship	UK	4,461	Sunk
15 Feb 17	*Brecknockshire*	Cargo ship	UK	8,423	Sunk
16 Feb 17	*French Prince*	Cargo ship	UK	4,766	Sunk
16 Feb 17	*Eddie*	Cargo ship	UK	2,652	Sunk
24 Feb 17	*Katherine*	Cargo ship	UK	2,926	Sunk
4 Mar 17	*Rhodanthe*	Cargo ship	UK	3,061	Sunk
10 Mar 17	*Esmeraldas*	Cargo ship	UK	4,678	Sunk
10 Mar 17	*Otaki*	Cargo ship	UK	9,575	Sunk in action
13 Mar 17	*Demeterton*	Cargo ship	UK	6,048	Sunk
14 Mar 17	*Governor*	Cargo ship	UK	5,524	Sunk

Armed Merchant Cruisers Which Served in the 10th Cruiser Squadron

Alcantara (Royal Mail): torpedoed 29 February 1916 in action
  with the raider *Greif*

Almanzora (Royal Mail)

Alsatian (Allan): squadron flagship

Ambrose (Booth)

Andes (Royal Mail)

Arlanza (Royal Mail)

Armadale Castle (Union Castle)

Avenger (ex-*Aotearoa*) (Union SS Co NZ): torpedoed by U-boat 14
  June 1917 in North Atlantic

Bayano (Elders & Fyffes): torpedoed by *U-27* 11 March 1915 off
  Galloway

Calyx (ex-*Calypso*) (Thomas Wilson)

Caribbean (Royal Mail)

Cedric (White Star)

Changuinola (Elders & Fyffes)

Clan McNaughton (Clan): foundered 3 February 1915

Columbella (Anchor)

Digby (Furness Warren): became French *Artois* on 25 November
  1915

Ebro (Royal Mail)

Eskimo (Thomas Wilson)

Gloucestershire (Bibby)

Hilary (Booth): torpedoed by U-boat 25 May 1917 in Atlantic

Hildebrand (Booth)

India (P&O): torpedoed by *U-22* in August 1915 off Norway

Kildonan Castle (Union Castle)

Mantua (P&O)

Moldavia (P&O): torpedoed by U-boat 23 May 1918 in English Channel

Motagua (Elders & Fyffes)

Oceanic (White Star): wrecked on Shetland Islands 8 September 1914

Ophir (Orient)

Orbita (Pacific SN Co)

Orcoma (Pacific SN Co)

Oropesa (Pacific SN Co): became French *Champagne* 2 December 1915; torpedoed by U-boat 9 October 1917 in Atlantic

Orotava (Pacific SN Co)

Orvieto (Orient)

Otway (Pacific SN Co): torpedoed by U-boat 23 July 1917 off West Scotland

Patia (Elders & Fyffes): torpedoed by *UC-49* 13 June 1918 in Bristol Channel

Patnea (Elders & Fyffes)

Patuca (Elders & Fyffes)

Teutonic (White Star)

Victorian (Allan)

Viknor (ex-*Viking*) (Viking Cruising): mined off Northern Ireland 13 January 1915

Virginian (Allan)

APPENDIX 3

Example of a T.124 Form

The several persons whose names are hereunto subscribed, being British subjects, and whose descriptions are set forth against their signatures, hereby agree with [name of RN officer] for and on behalf of the Lords Commissioners of the Admiralty to serve on board the said ship in the several capacities expressed against their respective names for any period not exceeding six months, but the Agreement to be terminable at a port in the United Kingdom after three months on either party giving seven days' notice.

(1.) The several persons whose names are hereunto subscribed agree that they shall be subject to the Naval Discipline Act:

(2.) Any offence committed by any such person shall be tried and punished as the like offence might be tried and punished if committed by any person in or belonging to His Majesty's Navy, and borne on the books of any of His Majesty's ships in commission:

(3.) Every such offender who is to be tried by Court-martial shall be placed under all necessary restraint until he can be tried by Court-martial:

(4.) On application made to the Lords of the Admiralty, or to the Commander-in-Chief, or senior officer of any of His Majesty's ships or vessels of war abroad authorised to assemble and hold Courts-martial, the Lords of the Admiralty, Commander-in-Chief, or senior officer (as the case may be) shall assemble and hold a Court-martial for the trial of the offender:

(5.) The officer commanding shall have the same power in respect of all other persons borne on the books or for the time being on board the same, as the officer commanding one of His Majesty's ships has for the being in respect of the officers and crew thereof or other persons on board the same:

(6.) The Naval Commander-in-Chief and senior Naval Officer in His Majesty's Service shall have the same powers over the officers and crew as if they have for the time being over the officers and crew of any of His Majesty's ships.

It is further agreed by the said [name of RN officer] provisions and clothing,* and allowances in connection therewith, will be issued according to the Regulations for H.M. Naval Service, and that in the event of death or injury caused by acts of the enemy pensions or gratuities in accordance with the Regulations printed on the last page hereof.

In witness whereof the same parties have subscribed their names on the other side hereof on the day specified against their respective signatures.

* Clothing is supplied to crews of Armed Merchant Cruisers only. In other ships, no uniform is required, and each person must provide his own clothes.

APPENDIX 4

Principles of Merchant Ship Construction

The construction of merchant ships follows completely different principles from that of warships. The latter are essentially weapon platforms and their purpose is to remain afloat and operational, whilst operating their weapons for as long as possible. To achieve this goal they have a high level of internal subdivision with many internal watertight compartments. Hull plating is strengthened with armour and a continuous weather-deck completes what is a strong box structure.

By contrast, merchant ships need lots of internal open space, with a minimum amount of subdivision, thus creating flexible stowage arrangements for cargo, or room to build accommodation for passengers. Merchant ships are also strong box structures, but with one essential difference. The weather-deck of a merchant ship is interrupted by large hatch openings, which render them subject to the ingress of large amounts of water in bad weather conditions if the integrity of the hatches is compromised.

To overcome the lack of internal sub-division in the armed merchant cruisers, large baulks of timber and large numbers of empty forty-gallon drums were stowed in the holds. These provided additional buoyancy in the event that the hull plating was breached by gunfire or torpedo. But the fact remains that merchant ships were unable, by the very nature of the principles of their construction, to stand up to damage caused by gunfire or torpedoes. They were also full of flammable materials. A lot was ripped out on conversion to AMCs but there was still more remaining than on many warships.

Andersons in the Shetlands, HMS *Dundee*

Name	Wife	Parent	Residence	Age	
Died					
Henry J	Ann Jane	Gilbert	Ulsta, Yell	36	Fourth cousin to Magnus John
Magnus John	unwed	Thomas and Mary	Cullivoe, N Yell	31	Fourth cousin to Henry J
Robert John	Barbara Arthurson	Janet	Nesting and Lerwick	35	No relation to any
Henry		Robert and Barbara of Huxter	Huxter, Whalsay	26	Brother to Robert
Survived and Decorated					
John G			Sodom, Whalsay		Second cousin once removed to Henry and Robert
Served					
Robert		Robert and Barbara of Huxter	Huxter, Whalsay	Died 1948	Brother to Henry

Second cousins
The children of two first cousins. They have a common great-grandparent.

Second cousins once removed
Two people for whom a second-cousin relationship is one generation removed.
The child of one's second cousin; also the second cousin of one's parent. One person's great-grandparent is the others great-great-grandparent.

Fourth cousins
Have a common great-great-great grandparent.

Select Bibliography

The following secondary sources have been consulted and were helpful in the writing of this book.

Abulafia D, *The Great Sea*, OUP (Oxford 2011)

Admiralty, *Naval Staff Monograph*, volume VII, September 1922

Bacon R, *The Concise Story of the Dover Patrol*, Hutcheson (London 1932)

Bennett G, *Cowan's War*, Collins (London 1964)

Cecil H and Liddle P, *Facing Armageddon, The First World War Experience*, Leo Cooper (London 2003)

Chatterton E K, *The Big Blockade*, Hurst and Blackett (London 1932)

Churchill W, *The World Crisis*, Thornton Butterworth (London 1923)

Corbett J S and Newbold H, *The Official History of the War: Naval Operations*, Longmans Green (London 1920)

Cruttwell C R M F, *A History of the Great War*, OUP (Oxford 1934)

David S, *100 Days to Victory*, Hodder and Stoughton (London 2013)

Davison R L, *The Challenges of Command: The Royal Navy's Executive Branch Officers, 1880–1919*, Ashgate (Farnham 2011)

De Chair D R S, *The Sea is Strong*, George G Harrap and Co (London 1961)

Devlin P, *Too Proud to Fight*, OUP (Oxford 1975)

Dunn S R, *The Scapegoat: the Life and Tragedy of a Fighting Admiral*, Book Guild (Sussex 2014)

George D L, *War Memoirs*, Oldhams Press (London 1938)

Hampshire A C, *The Blockaders*, William Kimber and Co (London 1980)

Herwig H H, *The First World War Germany and Austria 1914–18*, Bloomsbury (London 1996)

Hough R, *The Great War at Sea*, OUP (Oxford 1983)

Jane F T, *Jane's Fighting Ships of World War 1*, Jane's Publishing Company (London 1919)

Marder A J, *From Dreadnought to Scapa Flow*, volumes I, III, IV and V, OUP (Oxford 1965)

McLynn F, *1759*, Jonathan Cape (London 2004)

Oldys W and Birch T, *Miscellaneous works of Walter Raleigh*, OUP (Oxford 1829)

Osborne E W, *Cruisers and Battlecruisers*, ABC-CLIO (Santa Barbara 2004)

Petersen H C, *Propaganda for War*, University of Oklahoma Press (Oklahoma 1939)

Schmalenbach P, *German Raiders*, Stephens (Cambridge 1980)

Scrimgeour A, *Scrimgeour's Small Scribbling Diary*, Conway (London 2008)

Skalweit A K F *Die Deutsche Kriegsernährungswirtschaft*, Deutsche Verlagsanstalt (Berlin 1927)

Thompson J, *The Imperial War Museum Book of the Sea 1914–18*, Pan McMillan (London 2011)

Tuchman B, *The Proud Tower*, Hamish Hamilton (London 1966)

Tuchman B, *The Zimmerman Telegram*, Ballantine Books (New York 1958)

Tupper R, *Reminiscences*, Jarrold & Sons (London 1929)

Vincent C P, *The Politics of Hunger: Allied Blockade of Germany, 1915–1919*, Ohio University Press (Ohio 1985)

Watson A, *Ring of Steel*, Allen Lane (London 2014)

Newspapers and Magazines

Adelaide Chronicle
Brooklyn Daily Eagle
Daily Mail
Daily Telegraph
Dominion, NZ
Glasgow Herald
Hawera and Normanby Star
Liverpool Courier
Mariner's Mirror
Naval Review

Shetland News
Shipley Times and Express
Singapore Free Press and Mercantile Advertiser
Straits Times
Stornoway Gazette
Strand Magazine
Sydney Morning Herald
The Argus, Melbourne
The Economist
The Day, Connecticut
The London Gazette
The Press, Canterbury
The Shetland Times
The Times
Weekly Despatch

Other

Hansard online
Lilley, Terence Dawson (2012), 'Operations of the tenth cruiser squadron: a challenge for the Royal Navy and its reserves', PhD thesis, University of Greenwich

Further Reading

The interested reader may wish to also consult the following books.

Fayle C E, *Seaborne Trade,* John Murray (London 1920)
Spong H and Osborne R, *Armed Merchant Cruisers*, World Ship Society (Windsor 2007)
Woodman R, *More Days, More Dollars: The History of the British Merchant Navy*, vol IV, History Press (Stroud 2010)

Research Sources

The historical writer in the UK is blessed that the country possesses some of the best archives (and archivists) in the world. My thanks are due to the trustees and staff of the following organisations whose resources make the writing job both easier and more interesting. Primary sources consulted include those held at the institutions named below.

The National Archives, Kew
Imperial War Museum, London
Shetland Family History Society (Elizabeth Angus)
Shetland Museum and Photo Archive (Dr Ian Tait, Steven Christie)
Shetland Library (especially Douglas Garden)
The British Library, London
Churchill Archive Centre, Churchill College, Cambridge
National Maritime Museum, Greenwich
Hertfordshire County Council Department of Archives and Local Studies
National Museum of the Royal Navy, Portsmouth

Additionally, the online resources listed below have been helpful:

dreadnoughtproject.org
naval-history.net
wikipedia.org
JSTORarchive.org
firstworldwar.com

Index